THE DUST OF
HER SANDALS

THE DUST OF HER SANDALS

By

A. DE CASTRO ALBARRÁN

Translated by

SISTER MARY BERNARDA, B.V.M.

Mundelein College, Chicago, Ill.

NEW YORK, CINCINNATI, CHICAGO, SAN FRANCISCO

BENZIGER BROTHERS

PRINTERS TO THE HOLY APOSTOLIC SEE

1936

Nihil Obstat

ARTHUR J. SCANLAN, S.T.D.
Censor Librorum

Imprimatur

PATRICK CARDINAL HAYES
Archbishop of New York

NEW YORK, MAY 7, 1936

READER!

ANOTHER book about Teresa!

Many have been written, but that incomparable woman deserves them all, and for all of them the miracle of her life affords sufficient subject-matter, without being exhausted.

Mine is modest and unassuming, even in the name with which, on baptizing it, I have given it its affiliation with Teresa.

"Dust of Her Sandals. . ."

To the friends who know my devotion to Teresa, to those who know how many hours other studies about Teresa have occupied me for some years, it must seem strange that I now present this humble dust of the sandals of the nun. . .

There will be time for all, if God grant it.

For the present, I trust that all the hours which I have spent in gathering this dust have not been wholly idle.

At least they have not been idle for me. . .

And I confess that I have written these pages primarily for myself, just to write them, to delight and give pleasure to myself while writing them.

And this I have achieved.

While I was writing them in my leisure hours, I enveloped myself in the golden cloud of this blessed Teresian dust, and this cloud was as a calm and luminous retreat where body and spirit were comforted and rested from fatigue: from the fatigue of work and the weariness of life.

The book will hardly be without profit for you, Reader.

St. Teresa is great in her great deeds, but her greatness is, perhaps, better seen in her little deeds. This is what I offer you in this book: the little things of St. Teresa, *the dust of her sandals*.

All these stories of Teresa that I tell here, all

the sayings, all the information that I give you, although presented in simple prose, have as their authority some historic document. This suffices to give my narration the solidity of an objective base, which is enough for my purpose. I do not write with any object of criticism or polemics. He who wishes to enjoy these pages, be he devout or irreligious, must accept, above all, the traditional figure of the Saint, surrounded with her supernatural aureole.

Of the anecdotes or little stories that serve as the historic base for the narratives, some have been published already, but in appendices which only a few erudite admirers of Teresa read. I wish them to be more widely read, and for this reason I have withdrawn them from their obscurity and have brought them to light.

I have found others in long and laborious manuscripts, Teresian mines scarcely tried yet, especially among some of the processes made for the beatification and canonization of the Saint: in the *Espicilegio Historial* and in the *Memorias*

Historiales of Fray Manuel and Fray Francisco de Santa Maria.

At first I planned to gather in my book only those traces of the Saint which were wholly unknown, but finally I brought in others already familiar, to weave—very thinly, it is evident—the fabric of the principal stages of her life. This does not mean that the book is, even in the intention, a new biography of Teresa. It is not so ponderous nor so detailed. Perhaps it is similar, rather, to a series of clear and illuminating sketches.

I offer an agreeable innovation to my readers. As links that unite the narratives, I have copied some testimonies in praise of the Mother, given by the nuns who were her close companions, by the theologians who dealt with her intimately, or by men of authority who knew her.

This, simply, is what my pen offers in this book. It boasts neither of science nor of history nor of literature. Its intention has been to tap the underground spring in order that the hidden stream may leap and flow over the surface.

Drink the water, Reader. Enter within the little cloud of the dust of her sandals and let the dust penetrate the body and soul, for it is dust of life, of benediction and of glory.

THE AUTHOR.

CONTENTS

[11]

CONTENTS

[12]

CONTENTS

PART VI

A WOMAN RESTLESS AND ROVING

PART VII

"NOW THIS LITTLE BUTTERFLY IS DEAD"

THE DUST OF
HER SANDALS

DISCALCED

THIS blessed dust that we, on our knees, begin to gather, is the dust, the wake of light and of fragrance, that St. Teresa of Jesus left after her as she passed through life. Dust of her unshod feet.

One day during the Lenten season of 1563, Doña Teresa left the convent of the Incarnation. She went up the hill along the steep path that borders the wall. She came to the arch of St. Vincent.

Opposite the arch, on the other side of the road, is the Holy Basilica, reliquary of the martyrs Vincent, Sabina and Christeta. At the rear of the Basilica is the Virgin of the Grotto in her cave of rock.

Doña Teresa went down, fell on her knees before Our Lady and took off her shoes.

Already is she a discalced nun of Our Lady.

From this time the dust of her path will bear the blessed caress of her feet, and the feet of the Mother, through the poor sandals, will leave in the dust that they tread a virginal fragrance.

Dust of her sandals, dust of the bare feet of the Mother Teresa! . . .

There goes the Mother along her way. . .

After her a wind, wind that is the breath of the Holy Spirit, stirs up a whirlwind of dust.

The dust falls on the roadway in a shower of little stars of light, and each little star is a convent. And it falls as the snow on the mantles of her sons and of her daughters. It falls on the leaves of their books. It falls as manna on souls.

. . . And it falls now on the fortunate pages of my little book. . .

I.

A Beautiful Little White Butterfly

The childhood idyl of Teresa is the flitting about of "a beautiful little white butterfly."

She describes pleasantly in the Moradas *that silkworm which keeps growing until wings are born and it is transformed into a white butterfly. She, in her fluttering childhood, is this butterfly, white and winged.*

She was born with wings. And she was wholly white.

A crimson rose, the rose of martyrdom, attracts the white butterfly. She flies over the wall. But God does not wish that her wings be stained with the royal red of blood. More beautiful is her snow-whiteness that, little by little, love is tinging with crimson.

A blinding light has been enkindled. Round about her, under her own brightness, grow the flowers of evil, dazzling the sight. The little eyes of the butterfly waver for a moment, fascinated. But she does not approach so closely that the light singes her wings, nor does she rest for a moment on one of these flowers of fire. She passes above them, white and winged.

She has discerned other flowers, those that adorn Mount Carmel. . .

The Teresian Dawn

WITH the dawn she was born. Marvelous dawning! Four centuries have passed and the light of that daybreak has not yet grown faint in the obscurity of sunset. It burns each day more brightly, as sun-ray in the glory of a perennial noontide.

Her father, Don Alonso, inscribed on a bit of parchment that blessed date. The five lines are jubilant, as the joy of a great blessing. . . "On Wednesday, the twenty-eighth day of the month of March in the year fifteen hundred and fifteen, was born Teresa, my daughter, at five o'clock in the morning, a half-hour earlier or later, which was about day-break the above-mentioned Wednesday."

While she was being born it was "about day-break." But once Teresa was born, there was also born completely, suddenly, the day. . . A miraculous dawn illuminated the heavens. The stars—stars of sanctity, stars of glory—disappeared, vanished in the splendor of the new day. A fulgency, as of an aureola, crowned the tower of the fortress of Avila and spread above the embattled wall. Along the dusty roads of the two Castiles, in the thickets of ancient evergreen oaks of the Castilian pasture lands, among the olive orchards of Mancha, above the gleaming branches of the flowering orange groves of Andalusia, above the foamy crest of the waves of the sea, burned crimson lights, as tongues of flame of a new Pentecost of love. . .

And Mount Carmel, enraptured with sweet odors, flourished in a sudden springtide. . .

Teresian dawn! . . .

Teresa

WEDNESDAY of Holy Week, the fourth of April of the year 1515.

A great festival in the Monastery of the Incarnation, because this morning has been said the first Mass in its church.

A great festival, also, with much rejoicing, in the church of St. John, because they are baptizing the daughter of Don Alonso.

The priest who is baptizing her inquires of Vela Núñez, the god-father, what is to be the child's name.

Vela Núñez answers:

"Teresa."

Teresa! What a name! Teresa is not the name of a saint. . . If the father and godfather and priest could have foreseen that the child would become Mother Prioress and Mother

[25]

Foundress, certainly they would have chosen another name.

Imagine the distress of her nuns when they are going to celebrate the feast-day of their Mother and can not find *her Saint* in the calendar.

And Gracián, to tease her, on their way to make foundations, will joke her slyly:

"Your Reverence, my Mother, has not the name of a Saint."

And she hasn't, either. Teresa is not yet the name of a Saint. But it will be only a short while until it is the name of *the Saint.* . .

And this name is going to seem so beautiful to the Divine Lover that first He will join it with His own, and then, playing with it a strange juggling, will finish by taking it for Himself. . .

It is on the stairway of the Incarnation:

THE NUN: What is your name, my child?

THE CHILD: Why, what is the nun's name?

THE NUN: I, Teresa de Jesús.

THE CHILD: I, Jesús de Teresa.

Martyrdom

IN THE presence of Doña Beatriz, Rodrigo and Teresa are brought to judgment. They hang their heads as though they were two little thieves caught in the orchard. Their mother scolds them, because to run away from home causes much grief to God and to their parents. But their uncle, Don Francisco, defends them. He saw them, full of eagerness, hand in hand, climbing the hill of the Four Pillars, the road to the country of the Moors.

"We are going to the land of the Moors," says Teresa, "to ask for the love of God that they behead us there."

The face and the soul of the child are inflamed with an exquisite radiance. It is the fire, the crimson of blood, that dyed red the souls and the bodies of the martyrs.

But Doña Beatriz persists in condemning the

little brother and sister for their fault. Rodrigo is the more to blame on account of being older than his sister.

Rodrigo excuses himself:

"Teresa led me and made me take that road and kept saying that it was the shortest way for us to go to heaven."

The little head, the eyes of the child, agree; they assent to two things: that it was the shortest road to the enjoyment of the great blessings which, she has read, exist in heaven, and that it was she who urged her brother. Hers was the fault.

But let not the mother imagine that their leaving home was through lack of affection or of love.

She also gives her reason:

"When I saw the martyrdom the Saints endured for God, it seemed to me they bought very cheaply their going to enjoy God, and I wanted to die the same way."

Tears have begun to tremble in her eyes.

A BEAUTIFUL LITTLE WHITE BUTTERFLY

It is the sorrow of considering that now she will not be able to die in this manner.

To die thus: If she but knew! Because, thus, in this manner, she will die, consumed, as were the martyrs, in a burning fire. . .

But the fire that will consume her will be that of the flames of love.

Hermits

A CORNER of Don Alonso's garden, behind the wall, is the solitary desert of the hermit Rodrigo and the hermitess Teresa. In a corner there is a staunch and protective oak whose decayed trunk forms, level with the ground, an enormous opening like an ancient grotto. This is the cenobitical grotto of the hermits.

Since they have seen that it is impossible to go where they may be killed for God's sake, they have determined to become hermits, and in the hollow of the oak they have built their hermitage. Or, rather, they are building it now.

Rodrigo piles one above the other the little rocks that the gardener in his digging has heaped together, and Teresa pats on them handfuls of moistened earth that she brings from the recently watered garden.

Now the ceiling. Rodrigo cuts reeds and

divides them into equal strips. Teresa crosses them above the walls.

For the roof, the tall grass that grows near the well.

Already it is a hermitage.

Now for the grotto of the hermits, like the huts of the shepherds of Gotarrendura. At one side of the trunk, that of the hermit Rodrigo; on the other side, looking toward the Incarnation, that of the hermitess Teresa.

Teresa quickly cuts the last bundle of grass to roof her hut, because the sun is sinking.

"Finish quickly, Rodrigo, because now it is the hour for the reading."

Rodrigo, obedient as a good monk, stops at the command, with the handful of grass that he was going to place on his hut.

The hermitess has knelt before the hermitage and begins to read in the *Flos Sanctorum.*

The hermit, seated against the trunk of the tree, listens to her, enraptured. . .

The reading is that "punishment and glory shall be *for ever.*"

Teresa has read these fords, *for ever*, with a strange emotion. The childish voice of the little girl trembles with the grave solemnity of a monk of the desert.

"For ever, Rodrigo, for ever, ever, ever. . ."

Rodrigo, in a sweet enchantment, looks at the glowing eyes of his sister and repeats, charmed,

"For ever, ever, ever!"

The sun has set. A breeze becomes boisterous in the cluster of trees, and a little whirlwind is formed in the hollow of the decayed oak.

Rodrigo, at the sound of the stones that are falling, turns his head, startled. But Teresa takes no account of the fact that the breeze has destroyed the hermitage and has carried away the straw of the huts.

The two eternities, the eternity of punishment and the eternity of reward, have been opened to her eyes. And she is absorbed, as in an ecstasy, outside herself. . .

For ever, ever, ever!"

[32]

Virgin of Charity

IN THE hermitage of St. Lazarus, near the river, stands in her niche the Virgin of Charity.

On her knees before the Virgin, weeps Teresa, the daughter of Don Alonso.

Yesterday they carried Doña Beatriz, dead, in a long, narrow cart from Gotarrendura and buried her in St. John's church.

Teresa no longer has a mother. And she has not yet completed fourteen years. She realizes thoroughly what she has lost, and therefore has come here to see another mother.

With many tears she addresses the Virgin:
"Be my mother. Oh, be my mother!"

It seems that the sobbing of her petition is lost down the river in the murmur of the current, within the harsh noise of the mills.

The Virgin, motionless in her niche, moves neither lips nor eyes. But something must have occurred, because the little orphan, her prayer finished, has risen, resolute and encouraged, and on her forehead and on her face she feels a gentle and loving warmth, as though her mother had but just kissed her.

Games of Chess

Doña Teresa is sixteen years old.

You should see how she adorns herself and how she cares for her hands and how she perfumes her curls.

To keep the essences with which she perfumes herself, she has a golden pomander box.

She has little jackets with countless lacings.

She has skirts of fine scarlet cloth trimmed with black velvet.

She has little frocks and sleeves of varicolored damask velvet.

She has overskirts of purple damask and of black camel-hair and of yellow Rouen linen.

She has bracelets and rings and golden pendants and hoops of earrings.

She has a collar of pearls that is worth thirty thousand maravedi.

To make a fine appearance on the royal highway and in the pilgrimages of Sonsoles and Pancaliente, she has a pompous mule on which she rides proudly in a luxurious saddle with numerous fur-lined cinches.

To play chess she has a board fashioned of pieces of ebony and of silver, with figures of ivory. . .

. . . And she has a gallant cousin, who courts her. . .

. . . And she has—but this she does now know—she has another Lover Who has showered her with His gifts and Who pursues her. . .

Doña Teresa plays chess, but she does not realize the Lady checkmated, harassed and pursued, is she herself.

Let her play! Let her play! Let her flee and defend herself and fortify herself within a castle!

The King Who checks her is so skillful in the game that He will not be long in checkmating her. She will reveal it when she writes the sixteenth chapter of the Way of Perfection. . .

And, better still, when she bears, fastened within
the depths of her heart, the arrow of flame. . .
That will be the last checkmate in these games of
chess. . .

Seeking My Love

SEEKING her love. . .

The worthy neighbors of Castellanos de la Canada can not recover from their astonishment at this maiden who has come from the city.

When her sister, Doña María, spread through the village the news of her coming, there was endless consideration of the light-hearted temperament and the delightful disposition of Doña Teresa.

But now Doña Teresa is neither light-hearted nor talkative.

She is eighteen years old, and it seems as though she were continually thinking . . . thinking. . .

In the afternoon, especially, when the sun sinks beyond the hill of Penasalbas, Doña Teresa, a book in her hand, takes the road that passes by the very door of her sister's mansion and walks,

walks, in a state of absent-mindedness, when she realizes that she has lost sight of the village and has descended to the ravine of the river.

Two wolf-like mastiffs bark furiously in the glen, at the edge of a nomadic flock of sheep that is coming from Extremadura.

Doña Teresa shakes herself as though she were awaking, and turns her steps back up the hill toward the village.

Up the hill, up the hill! Oh, what a steep hill is that of this other interior way which the maiden is now ascending.

She goes in search of her love. . .

The fine books of romance which she read in the home of her uncle at Hortigosa have told her very gently that her love is not in those foolish idle pursuits with the cousins of Avila; they have told her that she must consider well whether perchance her love is as the little birds that sing up yonder in the most fragrant rose-bush of all Mt. Carmel. . .

Doña Teresa contends and struggles because in truth the ascent is painful. . .

But the disturbing voice that has pierced her inmost recesses, like a dart, harasses her, inexorable, constant, as a grievous martyrdom.

This afternoon the martyrdom breaks forth anew, like an interior fire that inflames her. The whole landscape, bathed sinisterly in the crimson light of this sunset, seems a cruel symbol. Those desolate crests of the Serrota de Villatoro. . . Those fierce summits of the *sierra* of Gredos.

O mountains, lofty mountains, mountains steep and wearying, like Mount Carmel! . . .

But this recurrent fury of the battle which increases in intensity may well be the forerunner of a victorious ending. . .

Those tormenting mountains that evoke the memory of the lofty peaks of Mount Carmel are, also, a tragic figure of Mount Calvary. . .

Mount Calvary, the most painful of all mountains!

The remembrance inflames Doña Teresa with ardor.

Up the hill to Mount Calvary climbed the Love of Loves. This Example well deserves that she climb to seek her love on the highest peak of Mount Carmel. If He endured such hardships for her, it is not much that she endure some for Him. . .

She will endure them. No longer is she a coward, nor is she afraid. Now the triumph comes. Already is heard the hymn of final victory:

Seeking my love,
I shall go over those mountains and shores,
I shall not gather the flowers,
I shall not fear the wild beasts,
And I shall pass the forts and frontiers.

II.

"Now the Flowers Are Opened"

The soul of Teresa must be a flowery paradise where every flower of sanctity will grow.

"Now the flowers bud forth; now they begin to yield perfume."

She has gone forth from her home on the way to the Incarnation, and when she tore herself from her father's arms the girl's heart has shed blood, like a victim. This blood—blood of sacrifice, blood of martyrdom—has watered the garden of her soul and made it fruitful. Her own heart is now a crimson rose.

The high walls of the Monastery protect the garden, as a shelter from the icy north winds. Jesus Christ, the Divine Sower, enters the enclosure at will, His hands full of seed. And when He raises His hands to bless, the seed falls, scattering. The springtide of the flowers begins.

That little white butterfly is now a bee that

makes honey. There are some drones that covet it, but the Divine Beekeeper puts them to flight.

The garden, the cloisters, the choir, the cells of the Monastery, are filled with the fragrance which Doña Teresa diffuses from her interior garden. Let the good odor cling to the other flowers of the Monastery. And the fragrance from the Incarnation will one day perfume all the gardens of Spain and the whole Paradise of the Church.

Two Teresas

THOSE two nuns who chat in the shade of the poplar tree in the garden of the Incarnation are called Doña Teresa de Ahumada and Doña Teresa de Quesada.

Two Teresas.

At just about this time a *holy* Teresa is to come forth from the Monastery of the Incarnation. Some nuns tell that a person with second sight has declared it. Others say that it is a prophecy of the holy Juan de Dios.

During the conversation, Doña Teresa de Ahumada says:

"Just think, Sister, they say that a holy Teresa is to come from this house; God grant that it may be one of us two, and that it may be I."

Doña Teresa de Quesada says:

"God grant that it may be I."

But Doña Teresa de Ahumada, after some

time had passed, ceased to be called Doña Teresa de Ahumada, and was called *Teresa de Jesús*.

In a Dark Night

THE nuns of the Incarnation would swear by the sign of the cross that at night fairies and witches walked in the Monastery. They do not swear it because their confessor has told them that believing in fairies and witches is a sin. But what is happening in the convent seems witchery.

A number of nuns had left their torn and ripped mantles in the choir, and all were found sewed and mended at dawn. And in truth the hands that sewed them must have been very excellent, because the mantles—glory be to God —have become like new ones.

And the greatest difficulty is that the marvel has been repeated many nights.

"Angels must have come down from heaven," has declared Catalina de Jesús, a lay-Sister who has revelations in prayer and a reputation of being very dear in the sight of God, because on one occasion when she arranged the feast of the Candles, they burned for a long time and all remained as entire as though they had not been lighted.

But another nun, very spiritual also, and extremely clear-sighted, has begun to reflect.

"There are angels in the Incarnation also, and there is no need of those from heaven to mend the mantles."

* * *

With the permission of the Mother Prioress, Doña María de Cepeda, cousin of Doña Teresa, and Doña Juana Suárez (her friend, will spend a while this night near a pillar in the shadow of an arcade of the cloister. This cloister upstairs is the passage to the choir from the oratory of Doña Teresa. If Doña Teresa is the angel who mends the mantles by night, she must pass along this way.

The Monastery has been submerged in the silent shadow of the night. Each little nun in her cell. Doña Juana and Doña María seek the darkest corner of the cloister. Now they are posted like two spies. Apprehensions that come with the murmurings of the trees in the garden brush them, and they tremble. They almost regret their adventure.

A slight creaking of a door that is opened cautiously. A circle of light, half extinguished in the obscurity, from a little oil lamp that advances along the cloister. Doña Teresa passes. The two nuns saw her lips move as she passed, but they did not hear the verses she was saying. . .

> "In a dark night,
> Inflamed with anxious love,
> O blessed lot!
> I went forth unobserved,
> My house being now in silence."

When Doña Teresa has passed the last arch and gone toward the choir, Doña Juana says to Doña María:

"There are angels in the Incarnation also. There is no need for those of Heaven to come down to mend the mantles."

III.

ANOTHER NEW BOOK. ANOTHER NEW LIFE

This new book and this new life at that moment in which the holy Mother, before the Virgin of the Grotto, in the Church of St. Vincent, joyfully bares her feet.

She is no longer Doña Teresa de Ahumada, but Teresa de Jesús.

A new name, a new life.

Christ is awaiting her at the door of St. Joseph. Teresa de Jesús comes, discalced, and Christ receives her in His arms. Christ has in His hands a crown; He puts it upon the head of Teresa.

The grating of the choir is closed. Within, the thirteen discalced nuns. A new life. In the midst of her daughters, the Mother.

"Come, my daughters, hasten to perform this task and weave this little cocoon, abandoning our self-love and our will. Let this worm die, let it die, as it does in accomplishing that for which

*it was created, and you will see how we behold
God and behold ourselves inclosed within His
greatness, just as this little worm is inclosed in its
cocoon. . ."*

*. . . The bobbin sings in the midst of the
group, the swift spindles dance, and on the
distaffs gleam the little bundles of flax.*

*María Bautista sews together two pieces of
coarse frieze to make herself a tunic, because it
seems to her that one of serge is but slight penance. She it is who has planted in the garden a
decayed cucumber well garnished with salt and
vinegar, and she does not doubt that it will
grow, because obedience has blessed this sowing.*

*The serge of the sheets is smooth and pliant
and the small straw mat is soft. The haircloth
and the discipline caress the penitent flesh.*

*In the refectory there are bread, cucumbers
and cheese, and if the food does not suffice for the
thirteen, the Lord has put tender and savory
shoots on the grapevine in the garden.*

The house is poor and indigent, so that it may

make but little noise when it falls. Those who are tall have to lower their heads in order not to strike the ceiling. When it snows the flakes fall through the holes in the worn-out roof tiling.

But this poor little house has two gate-keepers and guardians: at one door, St. Joseph; at the other, the Most Holy Virgin.

The Sermon

THE Saint esteemed preachers highly, provided they were not of those who prepare their sermons so that they may not give dissatisfaction.

She gathered together her daughters that they might be occupied in prayer for them, and when she heard sermons, never did she listen to a preacher so poor that she did not hear him with profit, even though, in the opinion of those who heard him, he did not preach well. If she saw that any one preached with fervor and zeal, she felt for him a special predilection.

But not all preachers reciprocated this approbation in regard to the Mother.

Here is one who thunders against her from the pulpit of St. Thomas in Avila.

We do not know him, because his name—may he be blessed by God—has vanished with the noise of his thunderings.

These are stormy days, in which the reformatory plans of the nun of the Incarnation keep the city excited and restless.

The friar shouts discordantly:

"Ill-doers are those nuns who for the sake of relaxation leave their monasteries with the excuse of founding new Orders. . ."

The two sisters, Doña Juana and Doña Teresa de Ahumada, are listening to the sermon.

The anathemas of the preacher descend from the pulpit like lightning, and crimson with shame the face of Doña Juana.

First, shame; then, anger and wrath.

Doña Juana can not endure further affronts.

She rises with a determination to leave the church. She intends not to stop until she reaches Alba de Tormes.

She looks for her sister.

But her sister, Doña Teresa, quite placid, is looking at the preacher and is smiling.

The Mother's Breath

DAY of mourning and day of gladness.

The Mother, seated.

On her knees, Gonzalo, her little nephew, son of her sister, Doña Juana.

The child is as though dead. The flesh of his little body has the color and coldness of a wax candle that is extinguished.

Doña Juana and Doña Guiomar weep, looking at him.

But Doña Teresa does not weep. She feels deep within her a marvelous warmth of life. Her womb is blessed by God that she may be the virginal mother of a glorious posterity of sons and daughters, a posterity that will never end. This maternity of hers has not yet begun, but Juan de Ovalle, the child's father, is helping her erect the little house, home for her daughters, that she can commence to be a mother.

Perhaps God wishes to repay Juan de Ovalle for his good services, granting that his holy sister begin now to be a mother . . . a mother who may give life to his little son.

Doña Teresa has bent over the face of the child. She has almost pressed her mouth to the rigid flesh of the little angel.

She breathes upon him: upon his face, upon his breast.

. . . Breath of Mother Teresa!

Breath of the Holy Spirit, Who, within her, breathes and lives!

. . . The child for some moments is wholly wrapped in the Mother's breath. . .

*   *   *

Another day, Doña Teresa and Doña Guiomar were alone.

And Doña Guiomar said to Doña Teresa:

"Sister, what about this? That child was dead; how is it that he lived?"

Other times, when Doña Guiomar spoke in this manner, Doña Teresa reproved her and asked her why she said those foolish things.

But this time Doña Teresa smiled and answered nothing. . .

She Plays

A GAME of the Mother with her daughters.

This game which the nuns of St. Joseph play now is for them the favorite game in their recreations.

They are in the garden and they play at being hermits and hermitesses, or, better, Teresas and Rodrigos.

The Mother, of course, is the hermitess Teresa when a child. The other nuns are the hermit Rodrigo who, poor fellow, has since died in the Indies. But Ursula de los Santos, Antonia del Espíritu Santo, María Bautista, Isabel de Santo Domingo, are now going to bring him back to life. . .

The garden of St. Joseph is, in the game, the garden of Don Alonso's home. And there is no need for the nuns to build hermitages for their game, because there in the garden are the hermitage of Nazareth, that of the Samaritan woman, that of the Risen Lord. . .

"And may the Lord be forever blessed and glorified," says the Mother, "for those hermitages were of little stones that fell down on us immediately, and these others do not fall upon us, because the hand of God and of the Most Holy Virgin sustain them."

The nuns in chorus respond.

"Amen."

The nuns surround the Mother in a group and all sit down at the door of the hermitage of the Samaritan woman.

The Mother searches in the *Flos Sanctorum* and says:

"Come, Rodrigo, because now it is the hour for the reading."

And she begins to read with a harmonious, very childlike voice.

When she has read *"for ever,"* the Mother stops and looks very tenderly at the nuns. . .

"For ever, Rodrigo, for ever, ever, ever! . . ."

The nuns, all with one voice, like the voice of a single child, repeat, charmed:

"For ever, ever, ever! . . ."

But now the game has been converted into reality. Again the two eternities, the eternity of the punishment and the eternity of the reward have been opened to the eyes of the Foundress, as they were opened to the eyes of the child in her father's garden, and now, just as then, she is absorbed as in an ecstasy, outside herself. . .

The candid voice of Rodrigo, which has become, after years, the voice of a discalced nun, is, in the glory of the ecstasy, an angelic music. . .

"For ever, ever, ever! . . ."

Doves and Dovecots

Doves from the dovecot of Gotarrendura.

Doña Teresa, in her cell of the Incarnation, tenderly remembers the doves of this dovecot.

It has snowed. Doña Teresa looks through the window of her cell. In the distance some little white doves that look like snowflakes, rise from the tower of St. Vincent and fly, worn and stiff with cold, above the battlemented wall, above the Monastery, toward the fulling-mills beside the river.

The thoughts of the nun wing their way, also, in a flock toward her little doves of Gotarrendura.

Doña Teresa tenderly loves the doves of this dovecot. The sacred memory of Doña Beatriz floats amid their cooings. Doves from this dovecot flew above her as she was going to be veiled at her nuptial Mass, "very richly attired in silk and gold." And they flew above her, too, when she was lying dead, in the long cart that brought her to Avila.

For that reason the doves are for Doña Teresa a dear remembrance of her mother.

And for that reason she loves them and cares for them devotedly.

Poor little doves, these snowy days! Their beaks will not find the little worm in the newly-plowed earth. They will be hungry.

Doña Teresa pities them and her solicitous and motherly pen writes:

> Señor Alonso Venegrilla: Please feed and take good care of the dovecot in these cold months, since it is well filled, and we shall be able to get something from it this year. Ask Señor Martín Guzmán for the beans and all that you need, for he will be very glad to give it.

> Written on the tenth of January, 1546.

> TERESA DE AHUMADA.

THE DUST OF HER SANDALS

Dovecot of Juan de San Cristóbal.

The Mother often looks at it from her cell in St. Joseph's. But the doves of this dovecot no longer awaken the remembrance of the little doves of Gotarrendura. Other doves now fly above the head of the Mother, for whom she has to make a dovecot. For that reason it is that she looks with so much worry toward this dovecot of Juan de San Cristóbal, which is so near St. Joseph's. And the fact is that the nearness of these doves pleases and delights the Mother. When they rest quietly on the tiled roof on sunny mornings, they are like other little nuns at prayer. Their plumage is white like the mantles of the discalced nuns. The ardor of their cooings enters through the lattices and fills the monastery with a gentle murmur. And this nuptial music that is diffused throughout the convent—one does not know whether it is the cooing of the doves from the dovecot, or whether it is the murmur of the nuns . . . psalter of the choir . . . the sigh of some nun who is enraptured in the little nest of her cell. . .

But every day the Mother thinks:

"Oh, how well this dovecot would serve, that in it might be reared these other little doves of the Virgin, who are my discalced nuns."

And one day Juan de San Cristóbal and Teresa de Jesús arranged the sale of the dovecot.

"Today, Quasimodo Sunday of this year of 1564, there was arranged between Juan de San Cristóbal and Teresa de Jesús the sale of this inclosure of the dovecot, for one hundred ducats, free from tithe and excise. They are payable in this way: ten thousand maravedi immediately, and ten thousand on the feast of the Holy Ghost; the rest on St. John's day of this present year."

Of the little old house of Juan de San Cristóbal's dovecot, the Mother made a hermitage with great devotion, the hermitage of the Lord bound to the pillar. . . The dovecot of Juan de San Cristóbal was finally converted into the little Dovecot of the Virgin. . .

Little dovecots of the Virgin, Our Lady.

The little dovecots of the Virgin numbered eight when the Mother gave them this name in the fourth chapter of the book of the *Foundations*. The Dovecots of St. Joseph of Avila, of Medina del Campo, of Malagón, of Valladolid, of Toledo, of Pastrana, of Salamanca, and of Alba de Tormes. And there still remained eight that the marvelous hand of the Foundress had to erect. Indeed this joyful and heavenly hand, when it is raised to bestow a blessing behind the grating of the locutory or beneath the oak-tree beside the road, is like a decoy-pigeon and a lure, which attracts doves and doves. . . She, traitorous dove, flies a little way with them, and then, in the midst of the Castilian plain, within the oak-grove of the pasture-ground, on the lofty peak of the *sierra*, she leaves for each flock a dovecot. . .

But all have the same name:

"The little dovecot of the Virgin, Our Lady."

A Strong Man

IT IS the Provincial who is speaking, and Báñez listens to him quite patiently.

This Father Provincial has never met Mother Teresa, but he has heard much of her ecstasies and of her books and of her experiences along the highways and in the road-side inns.

The Father General disapproves of it.

This is not the kind of life that St. Paul recommended to women. It would be better for the nun to stay in her convent cell, devoting herself to God.

The words of the Provincial enkindle the blood of Báñez in his veins but the good friar bites his tongue and keeps quiet through respect for his Reverence.

But indeed it is a great deal to keep silent.

The Father Provincial says:

"This nun will end in the Inquisition, like Sister Magdalena de la Cruz."

Báñez replies:

"Your Paternity is going to Toledo now, where she is; you will see her there."

They did not speak longer. The words of the friar theologian fell curt and sharp on the mind of the Provincial. They disturbed him a little, but they did not take away from him his asperity of temper toward the Mother.

*   *   *

The Lenten season passed.

The Provincial returned from Toledo. . . There he has seen Mother Teresa, who has given him kind greetings for her Father Báñez.

Báñez thanks him for the kindness and asks his Paternity:

"What does your Paternity think of Mother Teresa?"

His Paternity replies, saying:

"Oh, oh! You had me deceived; you said that she was a woman, and in faith, she is a real man, and one of full stature."

The Unfaithful One

THE old chronicles have charitably hidden the name of the nun of this story. But, in spite of that, the evoking of her memory was for many years, in the convent of Consuegra, a warning and a threat.

The incident was no less than a warning.

There was a nun with a black veil.

The veil is, for the discalced nun, the virginal garb that keeps the sacred purity of her betrothal. It is, furthermore, a perpetual mourning to remind her constantly that she is dead to the world. From the day on which the Carmelite takes the veil, her brows, her eyes, her countenance are reserved solely, jealously, for the eyes of the Beloved.

But it is evident that this nun did not well comprehend all the solemn majesty that the whiteness of her coif and the secrecy of her black veil placed upon her brow and her countenance.

One day the Mother met her. The nun had her face incompletely covered. The Mother seized the veil and pulled it vigorously as though to tear it from her. She did not tear it away, but the reproof was dreadful.

"A nun poorly veiled is like an unfaithful wife."

The nun, in the course of time, went to found Consuegra, and she herself told of her humiliation. Holy warning. In that Community, when a heedless novice twisted her coif a little above her brow, or raised her veil three fingers' breadth against the rule, the Mother Mistress, to correct her, used to say for the entire reproof:

"Remember, daughter, the unfaithful one. . ."

What a Foolish Prioress!

In a letter which the holy Mother wrote from Seville to her brother, Don Lorenzo, in the year 1571, she says at the end:

"I thought that you would send us that Christmas carol of yours, because these have neither feet nor head, and they sing it all. Now I recall one which I once made when I was feeling quite prayerful, and it seemed that I was more satisfied. They were . . . I do not know whether it was so, and in order that you may see that I wish to provide you amusement from here, I am sending it to you."

She copies three stanzas, and says:

"I do not remember any more. What a foolish foundress!"

This about the "foolish foundress" almost compels us to believe an episode that, she, laughing at herself, used sometimes to tell to María de San José. Little harm, since, in spite of the episode, we know her. We can, then, tell it without discredit to her.

It was that day of convent revolts, on which the Saint returned from St. Joseph to the Incarnation with the appointment as Prioress.

There was a mutiny stirring through the cloisters of the Incarnation. Neither the grave friars, nor the justices, magistrates and peace-officers who accompanied the Saint, succeeded in quieting the rebellious nuns.

Finally the bell of the Monastery rang for the Chapter, and the hundred and thirty calced nuns assembled in the Lower Choir.

Fretful faces and threatening gestures.

The Father Provincial read with serious and authoritative voice the letter of election.

Cries, protests, threats.

The Father Provincial inquires:

"Then, in short, you do not wish Mother Teresa de Jesús?"

[74]

But his voice is lost and drowned in the cry of the nuns.

Again, with stronger and more powerful voice, he inquires:

"Do you not wish Mother Teresa?"

A daring voice comes from amid the tumult.

"We wish her and we love her. *Te Deum laudamus.*"

There is a confused movement of the nuns, as of sparrows that have heard a shot.

Doña Catalina de Castro rises resolutely and takes the processional cross. Some, the majority, follow her and chant *Te Deum laudamus;* others remain and speak with acrimony of the Prioress and of him who sent her.

The Prioress is in the Church, clasping her statue of St. Joseph. When the crowd of nuns that Doña Catalina is leading enters, the Mother embraces the cross of her priorate. All go forth in procession from the Church and advance toward the choir.

The Mother Prioress enters the choir:

"What a foolish prioress!"

She has now forgotten that she is going to take possession of the chair of the prioress, and she sits down in her old seat.

When she realizes what she is doing, she can scarcely restrain her laughter.

But the device of which she makes use to conceal her forgetfulness is amazing.

She takes a statue of the Most Holy Virgin, places it in the chair of the prioress, seats herself at its feet, and says:

"This is the prioress!"

Eat, Daughter!

ANA de San Bartolomé saw it with her own eyes, and it was that day of sorrows, on which the Saint learned of the decree which the Nuncio had given to subject the discalced friars of the Reform to the Provincials of the Observants.

During those months of 1578 "the devil had become letter-carrier," and he flies swiftly, and daily and hourly he brings new evil tidings to the little dovecot of St. Joseph.

And one day he brought the worst of all the bad tidings: the notice of the Nuncio's decree.

The wrath of Monsignor Sega, that Nuncio of whom the Saint dared to say that "it seemed God has sent him in order to exercise us in suffering," had, finally, a furious recrudescence, and the lightning flash of its tempest was the unfortunate decree.

That day the holy Mother, weeping bitterly,

could do nothing but choke down the bitterness of her grief. Her sons, the sons of her great love and of her great suffering, were now delivered, bound hand and foot, to their executioners.

With this grief, the Mother had not been able throughout the entire day, to take a mouthful of food.

But at night, Ana de San Bartolomé who keeps her company in her sadness, begs her with many tears to go down to the refectory to break her fast before going to matins.

The Mother obeys.

Ana de San Bartolomé goes down to the refectory with her and sits down beside her.

The Mother is still weeping. Her tears moisten the bread which is on the napkin. Bitter bread. In it is filtered and concentrated all the bitterness of these tears.

But no, it is not bitter.

Jesus Christ, Who is right beside the Mother, now takes this very bread in His hands.

Ana de San Bartolomé sees Him.

And the nun sees yet more.

Jesus Christ breaks off a mouthful of bread and places it in the mouth of the Mother.

And He says to her:

"Eat, daughter, for now I see that you are enduring much; take courage for it can not be less."

IV.

THE INTERIOR CASTLE

Christ fashioned with His own hands the diamond and the crystal. And He has made of Teresa's soul an interior Castle which in the dark night is resplendent as a precious stone, large and clear. The torch of the Lamb always illuminates this Castle, the same as the City of Glory. And its seven mansions are illuminated by the same light . . . the Love that burns night and day in the nuptial chamber. Because of this the Castle is, in its entirety, a brazier and a flame.

Teresa de Jesús is imprisoned in her own Castle. A prisoner, and at the same time free and jailor.

> This divine prison
> Of the love with which I live
> Has made God my captive
> And my heart free. . .

For it is here that a ladder rises to Heaven from the battlements of the Castle. By it Teresa *ascends and expands the wings of her spirit above the peaks of Glory.*

And by it God descends to the Castle.

And one day descends also a cherub who bears in his hands a dart of gold and of fire.

God Walks Among the Pots and Pans

COOKING and praying agree with each other. For the discalced nuns of St. Joseph the kitchen is also an oratory. As there are no lay-Sisters in the Community, the choir-Sisters, with great contentment of spirit, sweep and scrub and cook.

The Mother Teresa, Foundress and Prioress, also cooks in the kitchen when her turn comes. Indeed, she has among the nuns the reputation of being a very skillful cook. She has commanded that whatever God may give them to eat shall be well prepared, and she wishes to be foremost in fulfilling the rule.

How the Mother enjoys preparing the poor food for her daughters. And how sumptuously the daughters fare with the poor food that has passed through the Mother's hands. The boiled squash and the carrot salad have then a different flavor.

[85]

Still, it seems that when she goes into the kitchen, God is more mindful of the poor Discalced of St. Joseph. The neighbors come more often to the turn with oil and with eggs, and even preserves frequently appear, sent by other nuns of neighboring convents.

In spite of all this, the nuns are not very tranquil the week that the Mother cooks.

The most disturbed is Isabel de Santo Domingo.

And the reason for this uneasiness on the part of Sister Isabel is an ecstasy that the Mother has had.

The ecstasy occurred in this way.

One time the Mother was frying a little oil in the frying pan. She was frying and praying.

"God also walks among the pots and pans," thought the Mother. And, with the frying-pan in her hand, she was enraptured in God.

The frying-pan shook in the hand of the ecstatic cook, and the oil shook in the frying-pan.

It was the providence of God that at this moment Isabel de Santo Domingo entered the kitchen and, seeing the Mother motionless, rushed toward her and took the frying-pan from her hand.

When the Mother came to herself, Isabel de Santo Domingo ventured to say to her:

The next time, my Mother, before becoming enraptured, remember to see whether there is perhaps no more oil in the house besides that which is in the frying-pan, as was the case just now. Consider what would have happened if it were spilled on the floor."

The Mother smiled and replied:

"Remember, my daughter, that God always walks among the pots and pans."

From that day, when the nuns mentioned the Mother's great skillfulness in cooking, Isabel de Santo Domingo used to add:

"But God deliver us from her becoming enraptured while holding the frying-pan in her hand when we have no more oil in the house."

Flowers

God has blessed the convent garden and everything has flourished.

Mother Teresa has gone down to the garden.
The Spouse has entered
The delightful garden desired. . .

The garden of St. Joseph of Avila hides behind the high wall with its little hermitages, the hermitage of the Samaritan woman, that of the Risen Lord, that of the Lord bound to the pillar, and each one of them is, in the peace of the afternoon, a monastic haven.

But this afternoon Mother Teresa does not enter to pray in either the hermitage of the Samaritan woman or in that of the Risen Lord. She has seated herself on the thick grass at the edge of the irrigation channel along which the water flows.

Now she is writing, in the book of the *Life*,

about the four kinds of prayer, and this afternoon her best prayer, the most inspired, is this:
to watch the water flow.

It is here that María de San Francisco inter-
rupts her in her prayer.

She carries in her hand a cluster of white lilies
and has her scapular overflowing with lilies, poppies and immortelles.

She offers her treasure to the Mother. The
Mother thanks her for it.

"May God repay you for it, my daughter, who
bring me so great a gift."

And the Mother's hands, two virginal lilies,
arrange in wreaths and in clusters the lilies, the
silvery marguerites and the purple poppies.

"The flowers, my daughter, give me much
pleasure, for I consider that my soul is a garden
and that the Lord walks within it and cuts the
flowers that He wishes. . ."

The Mother has stopped in an attitude of listening. . .

. . . My soul a garden . . . and the Lord walks within it. . .

She has perceived Him! She has felt Him!

In the garden of her flowering heart walks the Gardener. . .

And she perceives the sound of His footsteps among the flowers. She feels the caress of His hands that cut them.

> I stayed and I forgot myself,
> I reclined my head upon the Beloved,
> Lost to all things and to myself,
> Leaving my cares
> Forgotten among the lilies.

The Sermon of Fray Domingo

FRAY Domingo Báñes is preaching to the nuns of St. Joseph.

Seated near the grating in the friar's chair, the doctoral voice of the Dominican has an amazing gentleness. It seems that his lips, at other times harsh and austere, are now anointed with oil and honey. Throughout the speech the words tremble with a fatherly emotion.

Within, on the other side of the grill, are dimly perceived the shadowy forms of the nuns. Hardly does a little cough, abruptly checked, gentle, shatter for a moment the sacred quiet of the ambient air, like the wing of a sparrow that, passing above the surface in its flight, grazes the crystal of the lake. . .

Suddenly, within, a deep moan, long, delightful. . .

It seems a groan from the Mother Teresa! . . .

A silent movement of nuns.

Fray Domingo cuts short the sermon and rises. He takes off his cowl. He bows his head and clasps his hands before his breast as if he were adoring. . .

There is a solemn silence of religious fear. In the air, the sound of wings of seraphim. God is felt.

Finally the frightened voice of a nun is heard near the grill:

"You should not have risen, my father. It is passing from the Mother now."

Fray Domingo Báñes replies:

"I shall never remain seated while the Mother is enraptured. When these raptures seize her, God is within her, and I adore Him. . ."

The Mother Sleeps

AN HONORABLE office is that which Isabel de
Jesús María holds in the Community. She is the
awakener of the Mother.

With her eight years, she is active and bright.
She is, furthermore, the sister of Father Gracián.

Since the Mother with her own hands put on
her the holy habit in Toledo, she has loved her
deeply. When a nun reproves her for some slight
mischief the Mother comes to her defense:

"Let no one scold my Belita, who does more
than enough. . . What more would you wish of
a little girl, who makes stockings bigger than she
herself?"

After this, Isabelita does not detach herself
from the Mother's side.

But we are saying that she is her awakener.

When the Mother wishes to sleep, she calls the
child and says to her:

"Belita, take this hour-glass and sit here beside me. When you see that I am asleep, turn the glass, and, when a quarter of an hour has passed, awaken me."

And the Mother falls asleep.

Over the room falls solemnly the entreaty of the Spouse:

". . . I adjure you, O ye daughters of Jerusalem, by the roes, and the harts of the fields, that you stir not up, nor make the beloved to awake, till she please."

But the hour-glass begins to pour silently its little heap of sand.

And the Spouse again entreats:

"Cruel lions of the forest,
  Crouching in their secret lair,
Fawns and does so wild and restless,
  And all the birds of the air.
Nightly terrors that alarm us,
  Gloomy valleys, lowly plain,
Burning heat and lofty mountains,
  Howling winds and driving rain.

[94]

"By the music of the viols,
    By the siren's soothing strain,
I adjure you and command you
    From your fury to refrain.
Cease your clamors, come not nigh us,
    At a distance still abide,
And occasion no disturbance
    Of the slumbers of the bride."

But Isabelita, faithful to her charge, awakens the Mother:

"Mother, the quarter of an hour has passed."

The Mother awakens and smiles.

"Why, child, it is not possible that so much time has passed."

The child insists that it has and the Mother obeys.

If it were not for the fear that it might be discovered what kind of dreams are hers, the Mother would answer in another manner. . . In that manner in which she once answered a nun when the latter aroused her from an ecstasy:

"May God forgive you, my daughter, and don't let it occur to you to awaken me again."

[95]

May My Eyes Behold Thee

THE third day of the Easter-tide. As this is the first Easter that the little dovecot of Salamanca rejoices, Mother Teresa wishes that her daughters be happy and merry. These days they are spinning in haste to make two mantles and thus be able to return to the Fathers of the Company those two that Brother Bartolomé brought them as a loan that night of All-Souls on which they came to the foundation. It is known, indeed, that in the chatter of recreation, the spindle makes fewer turns and the bobbin stops more frequently, but let the holy Fathers wait another little while, for on these festival days of Easter it is right that the nuns have a while longer for merriment.

As the night is so beautiful, mild and clear, the Mother has left them to go out to the garden.

The circular space under the grapevine-arbor is animated. Amid the chatter is heard, also, the clatter of the bobbin turning about. The white balls of flax dance, interweaving their threads. The nuns, too, especially the novices, come out into the center and dance and clap their hands and sing and laugh. The Mother laughs also, and makes merry, but what can be the matter with Mother Teresa this Easter-time, for even amid the wrinkles of her laughter, the little cloud of a betraying sadness does not cease to float? "All day she has been so lonely that, except when she received Communion, she has had no realization that it is the feast of the Resurection."

More than anyone else, Isabel de Jesús, the Segovian novice who came to receive the habit from the Mother's hands, has noticed the Mother's sadness. What would she do to cheer her?

Her sweet and harmonious voice is set free like the singing water of a rivulet.

> Let my eyes behold Thee,
> Sweet, good Jesus,

Let my eyes behold Thee,
Then let me die!

Alas! Sister Isabel does not realize what she has sung! The song has been a keen sword that has pierced the Mother's soul.

As the arrows leap whistling from the strong and firm bow, from the hymn of the novice must have rushed strange arrows that have plunged into the Mother and have wholly trans-pierced her. . . Let my eyes behold Thee! . . . No, her eyes do not behold Him yet, because she is not yet dead. The anguish of not dying is so strong and so insufferable that it has cleaved within the soul as a dagger, and the soul "is dy-ing to die." And the pain is so deep and so intense that it enraptures.

Transported, divinely entranced, the Mother has fallen into the arms that her daughters have extended to her.

Four nuns carry her inert body to her cell. The cell has a window on the garden. And on the grating of the window, some rays of moonlight that have been dancing like the strings of a lyre, gather the murmur of the rosebushes of the garden and sing very sweetly:

> "I live, but yet I live not in myself,
> For since aspiring to a life more high
> I ever die because I do not die."

The Gift of the Lance

THE lance of the transfixion was the "severe, delightful martyrdom" of the Mother. When she felt it in her innermost being, "the pain was so great that it compelled her to utter moans. . ."

This night, praying matins in the choir, the pain of love has stricken her so severely that each psalm of the breviary has been a distressing groan.

The clear voice of the nuns has chanted sweetly:

"As the hart panteth after the fountains of water; so my soul panteth after Thee, O God."

But the voice of the Mother Teresa, when she wished to chant this verse, has been broken by a deep sob, for within her soul have been enkindled suddenly "desires for God so intense and so acute that they cannot be told."

These longings for God, relentless and delightful, are a bundle of arrows of fire, thrust, as into a quiver, within the depths of the Mother's soul. Tonight the recital of the breviary is for the nuns a constant temptation to distraction. The more learned, when some verse comes that they know by heart, raise their eyes from the breviary and avail themselves of the opportunity to look at the face of the Mother Pioress, without ceasing to chant.

Ana de Jesús, particularly, feels a great scruple on leaving the choir, because sometimes she has been distracted through the entire psalm, her eyes fixed upon the divine glow of the Mother's face.

And as she knows of the gift of the lance, years ago, in this very choir and at the home of Doña Guiomar, she has thought to herself: "The cherub with the lance is probably not far away now."

* * *

All the convent of the Incarnation has fallen asleep. In the peace of the night, the distant wall softens the echoes of the city and there comes to the Monastery only the sound of the water that sings amid the willow-trees of the nearby gardens.

The nuns are sleeping; but Ana de Jesús does not sleep. In a pleasant restlessness she thinks that she sees the Mother, glowing and heavenly as she saw her in the choir. . .

But no, she does not see her. . . Suddenly the nun trembled from head to foot, on the bed of straw. . .

An "Ay!" deep, very troubled, extremely sorrowful, has come quivering through the air, like an arrow . . . more exclamations, more moans, very sweet and very anguished, as though they were the complaints of a loving martyrdom. . . And they come—there is no doubt of it—from the cell of Mother Prioress, which is beneath that of Ana.

*　　*　　*

Now Ana de Jesús is at the door of the prioress' cell. She opens the door.

In the middle of the cell is the Mother, on her knees. With her hands upon her heart, she is a pure flame. She sighs, and with each groan it seems that the soul is being torn from her. . .

Ana de Jesús, who, terrified, has remained at the door, sees no more. But yonder, near the Mother on the left side, has descended in a sweep a little cherub, "very beautiful," and so glowing that he seems a flame. . . He raises high in his hands a long dart of gold and on the tip of the dart burns a crimson flame. Now the cherub, as if he were a soldier armed with a lance, discharges with the dart at the Mother a strong blow that goes straight to her heart. And through the center of the heart, the arrow pierces the very innermost part, clear to the living center of the soul. The pain is so great that the Mother cries as though out of her mind; and the sweetness of this anguish is so excessive that with her very groans she is pleading that it wound her still more. The pointed weapon burns her "as a living thorn plunged into the substance of the spirit"; it burns her in the inmost center of the heart of her soul, as if it were "a grain of mustard, very minute, very intense, and very much inflamed"; and, with the burning, the Mother is wholly consumed with love. And this singular soldier of love is so cruel that instead of drawing out the dart immediately, now that it has made the wound, she twists it within the wound, as one who seeks for fuel in order to increase the flame. . .

He draws it out finally, but coming out, as though it were barbed with prongs it seems to tear the innermost depths and bring them with it. . .

And Mother Teresa, in a transport of anguish and of glory, enraptured, transfigured, keeps delighting in unusual enjoyment of love's sorrow.

> "O gentle hand and touch,
> O wound in sweetness rife,
> O burning, a foretaste
> Of everlasting life.
> The debt is paid that long was due,
> And death by death brings life anew."

Ana de Jesús has recovered a little from her amazement. Now she is kneeling close to the Mother. And again she repeats the only thing she knows how to say:

"What is happening to you, my Mother?"

And this time, the Mother, turning her head a little, looks at her very sweetly and replies:

"Go, my daughter, and may such a thing happen to you."

Relic and Reliquary

AFTER the transverberation, Mother Teresa is suffocated with a divine warmth.

The wounds of the soul, when they are so deep and so intense as those which this glorious dart has opened within the Mother, end finally in the marvel of unusual outgrowths that appear on the very flesh of the body.

And the red-hot coals of fire that have been inflamed in the deep center whither the point of the lance reached, are casting toward the exterior, sparks, flashes, that overflow upon the face, upon the forehead, upon the breast, upon the hands. . .

The Mother is completely enveloped in the live coals of a divine fever.

So overcome and fatigued that she can do no more, she has let herself fall upon the oaken bedstead.

"Daughter! Daughter! Open the window for me!"

The Mother calls the daughter of her soul, Ana de Jesús.

Before, when Ana came down from her cell on hearing the cries, the Mother commanded her to leave, but she remained at the door of the cell. From here she has heard the summons.

She opens the window wide. She also opens the lattice.

"The peaceful night," a night of stars and of perfumes, enters suddenly through the open window. "The air of the battlements, air of the dove flight," envelops in its freshness, as in a caress, the burning face of the Mother and plays with her hair, damp with perspiration.

But the Mother still complains:

"I am burning up, daughter, but what heavenly heat! I should like to see you ill of this complaint as I am now."

In spite of this, Ana would prefer to cure the Mother.

"What could I give you, my Mother, that would heal you?"

The Mother feels on her forehead all the heat of this celestial fever. Her hair, now white, seems the crest of flames from a fireplace. And beneath this fire, her head is burning.

Again she seeks from her daughter some relief. "This hair, my daughter, is burning my head. It will give me relief to cut it."

A sudden delight makes the breast of Ana de Jesús tremble, and her face is illuminated with joy. She takes the scissors.

She puts her hand on the Mother's head and caresses her snow-white tresses. They burn. These snowy tresses burn as if they were filaments of flame or rays of the sun itself.

The nun's hand trembles as she cuts the first lock of hair. She trembles all over. But she trembles with reverence and with delight. . .

And she entertains herself with a secret thought:

"I have a relic. With this hair, I now have a relic of my holy Mother."

But the Mother awakens her from her thoughts:

"Why are you thinking such foolish things!
Now I command you to throw it in the rubbish-
heap."

And, confused, almost without realizing what
she says, Ana de Jesús exclaims:

"God help me! What a reliquary for such a
relic!"

But the Mother no longer replies, because she
has begun to woo the Beloved:

> "We will go in early morning
>   While the dew is on the ground,
> To the garden where the flowers
>   In their beauty may be found;
> And will make a garland of them
>   In which emeralds shall shine
> Knit and bound and held together
>   By a single hair of mine."

> "By that single hair that fluttered
>   On my neck and seen by Thee—
> Thou didst look again upon it
>   And wert by it drawn to me.
> Thou wert made a willing captive,
>   Weak and slender though it be,
> And I dared to look upon Thee
>   And in looking wounded Thee."

Transfiguration

THE Mother rests from her journey in the convent of Valladolid. Her faithful companion, Ana de San Bartolomé, rests with her also.

But Ana, with the care of awaking the Mother, has arisen very early. She has risen before the dawn. It grieves her to deprive the Mother of sleep so early, but she must obey. She goes out silently from her cell.

The monastery sleeps.

The nun advances in the darkness to the cell where the Mother sleeps, and opens the door.

The cell is completely inundated with light. It is not the light of the sun, that enters through the window. The window is closed and the sun has not yet risen. Or rather, it seems as though it were rising right here in the cell, from among the clothes of the bed, where the Mother is lying. Better still, the Mother is the sun. Her face, her hands, her entire body, shine through the worn coverings, as though they were of illuminated crystal. The coarse serge of the sheet that covers her, with its old patches, is a white cloud tinted red. . .

The cell sends forth the fragrance of gardens. . .

And in the marvel of this transfiguration, the Mother sleeps.

Ana de San Bartolomé kneels beside the bed and prays.

Scattering a Thousand Graces

SIERRAS and mountains, the harsh *sierras* and the wild mountains of Ubeda. Blue distances of the Sierra Morena. An endless panorama, set with peaks of emerald and of gold. A sun that diffuses itself in blinding torrents over the majestic and perfumed landscape. Luminous May. Sound of water, birds and flowers. . .

Under the trees of the poplar-grove, through which the river crosses, the six nuns who left Veas this morning, accompanying the Mother Foundress.

Antonio de Gaytán, Gregorio Nacianceno and Julián de Avila chat freely in a leisurely walk.

Among them all they have taken good care of the provisions they brought from Veas: boiled eggs, honey and preserved pumpkin.

Now to the carts again, for the road to Seville is long.

But the Mother Foundress is missing.

"We shall not be able to get her away from here," says María de San José, "for with this variety of flowers and the singing of the little birds, she is wholly occupied in praises of God."

It is the truth, the Mother has withdrawn from the group and is alone, half sitting, half kneeling, near the trunk of a poplar tree that waves its branches above the water of the river.

Twice María de San José has gone to ask her when they are going to resume the journey. But she has barely replied.

"Leave me alone, my daughter."

Now Julián de Avila, a bit ill-humored, is going to seek her.

The grass, deep and soft, deadens the sound of his footsteps, that is lost in the music of the poplar grove. The grove is a hive of insects that hum and a haunt of birds that sing.

The Mother has not heard the footsteps of the good chaplain, nor does she notice that he is coming.

Nor does he finish approaching the Mother; he does not dare.

"Oh, God help me, what a nun!"

It is evident that she is at prayer. But it must be a very lofty prayer, for she is motionless and quiet, as though dead. From her eyes comes forth a glorious radiance. Round about her the illuminated ambient is a halo of sanctity. And in the green grass, the smiling daisies and the golden bell-flowers form about the Mother a garland of stars and of flowers.

It seems that she asks:

"O ye trees of trackless forests,
     And ye thickets of the land;
Shade and shelter for the weary,
     Planted by His loving hand.
O ye meadows, fresh and verdant,
     Pictures of the land above,
Decked with flowers bright and fragrant
     Tell me, have you seen my Love?"

[114]

THE INTERIOR CASTLE

It seems that they answer her:

"We have seen Him! we have seen Him!
  Oh! the beauty of His face!
Moving through the groves, and pouring
  Down the treasures of His grace.
Hastening on, He looked upon them—
  Oh! that look! how full of love—
And the groves became more lovely
  With a beauty from above."

V.

SHE BECAME A WRITER

She obeyed and she wrote. Obedience placed the pen in her hand and upon her pen rested the Holy Spirit.

"Why do they wish me to write?" she used to say. "Let the learned ones who have studied write, for I am a simpleton and I shall not know what I am saying. There are enough books written on matters of prayer. For the love of God, let me spin my distaff and follow my choir and the duties of religion, like the other Sisters; for I am not fit for writing, I have neither the health nor the head for it."

But she surrendered her will and "became a writer." And "with the passing of time," instead of spinning with the bobbin, at times she used to spin with the pen. The thread was then the silken fibre of her thought and of her love. Like the silkworms that "spin from themselves,"

Teresa, when she writes, also spins from her very self, spins from the measure of light in her soul.

So the Book of the Life *is "her soul," and the* Interior Castle *of the* Mansions is her own Interior Castle.

But the soul of Teresa is divinely elevated.

For this reason, when she pours herself throughout her books, there is a divine and celestial effusion. As God is within her soul, God speaks and Teresa writes. While she writes, a marvelous splendor envelops her body, like the glory of a transfiguration. It is the reflection of the divine that rushes from her soul to her pen. She writes quickly, in haste. Someone moves her hand and her pen. Perhaps on beginning, "she takes the paper like a foolish thing that knows neither what to say nor how to begin," because "just as the birds that are taught to speak do not know more than they are taught or that they hear, and repeat this many times, so does she follow the letter." But the voice of the Master Who dwells within her sounds, remote

*and calm, and the echo of this voice makes the
pen of the Doctor tremble. And the stream of
wisdom flows over the sheet of paper.*

Above the book flutters the Holy Spirit.

My "Life"

FATHER Martín Gutiérrez, Rector of the
Company in Salamanca, has been ill for some
days. It is probably the effects of that fever
which, in the last months of 1569, devastated the
College of San Blas.

As he has consoled Mother Teresa so much,
now the Mother is going to console him.

She is little pleased that her *Life* should pass
from hand to hand, especially after the warning
in connection with the Princess of Eboli. The
book was "her soul;" it was not right that *her
soul* should go about constantly handled.

But this good Father Martín has well deserved
this expression of friendship. Furthermore, this
will be the best way for him to enter completely
the *Interior Castle* of the Mother's soul. Reading her book, he will know her better.

As the Father is now relieved after the fever, Brother Bartolomé Pérez, seated at the head of the bed, begins to read. . .

"The voice of the brother, more and more moved, is opening, as with a key, the doors of the *mansions*. . . The Father's bed, the whole room, is enveloped in a divine aroma, is illuminated, is inflamed. But particularly are the eyes of Father Martín illuminated and his heart inflamed. . ."

"Be quiet now, Brother!"

Father Martín has remained as though beside himself, in a quiet, ecstatic rapture.

When he again recovers consciousness, he sighs with a deep moan that seems to return to him his soul. . .

And inflamed, tremulous, he says to Brother Bartolomé:

"You probably do not understand this that you are reading, Brother; for they are things of such a nature and from a soul so elevated in spirit that it is necessary to feel them first in order to understand them."

The Brazier

FRAY Diego de Yanguas is a famous lecturer on theology. He is now at the Dominican convent of the Holy Cross in Segovia.

Since the first occasion on which he heard the confession of Mother Teresa, he has felt such great reverence for her that just to give Communion to her he goes often to say Mass for the discalced nuns in the rented house that the Mother has converted into a convent.

And now the Mother knows it, and all the nuns of the Community know it. . . At break of day when Fray Diego comes, he first hears the Mother's confession; the confession finished, he asks her for the book of the *Life*, he remains reading for some time, and then he says Mass.

The nuns, curious, now begin to conjecture: "Why must Fray Diego read every day before Mass the Mother's book? Someone who knows about the other book on the *Canticles,* which the Father commanded her to burn, has begun to fear maliciously. . . Perhaps he will end by commanding her to burn the book of the *Life,* as well.

But Fray Diego has remarked to a nun:

"The Mother says rightly that this book is *her soul,* and she also says truly that her soul is like a brazier where are poured out fragrant perfumes; there is seen neither the light nor where it is, but the heat and sweet-smelling smoke penetrate the entire soul, and even the body frequently shares it."

That day he did not say more.

But another day, importuned by the Mother Prioress, he was affected in a wholly paternal manner, and ended by giving the entire reason:

"When I wish to arouse my ardor in order to say Mass, I do nothing but take the brazier. And the brazier is the book of the *Life,* because in this book is the soul of the Mother, which is a pure flame."

The Castle of Clear Crystal

A SNOWFALL that has blotted out the roads through the whole Moraña has detained the travelers at the inn of Arévalo.

There has stopped at the inn, also, Fray Diego de Yepes, who is going to Zamora, and the Mother Teresa de Jesús, who, with three other nuns, is making the journey from Medina to Avila.

But on the third day a clear sun dawned on the snowfall, and the guests saddled their beasts and, one after another, were leaving the inn.

Fray Diego de Yepes and the Mother take leave of each other.

The Mother says to Fray Diego:

"How I forgot myself last evening with you; I do not know how it happened. These desires of mine and the affection I feel for you have made me forget prudence; would to God that they may have brought me profit."

Fray Diego promised the Mother to keep her secret while she should live, and each went his way.

Fray Diego kept his promise and did not reveal the secret while the Mother lived, but "after she died, he did not wish to leave a soul to whom he did not publish it."

*   *   *

The secret of Fray Diego was that which the Mother confided to him that snowy afternoon at the inn of Arévalo.

The Mother with her nuns has spent the entire day in the retirement of their room.

Fray Diego, like a faithful porter, has been diligent in sending to the kitchen the maids and the muleteers. He allows entrance to no one, unless there be necessity. But he inwardly feels a tremendous desire to enter to speak to the Mother.

Finally he asks her permission and the Mother grants it.

Fray Diego enters Mother Teresa's room.

The room is secluded and austere, like a cell. The rough conversation of the muleteers who are warming themselves in a group at the kitchen fire does not penetrate here. In the cell, a modest window. The little window has two bars that cross each other, and through it filters the softened light of the snow.

In the middle of the room glows a little brazier of earthenware that the inn-keeper brought. Near the brazier the friar and the nun are talking. Or, rather, the nun speaks and the friar listens.

In her conversation Mother Teresa becomes more and more inflamed, and her words rush forth vehement and glowing like sparks of fire. Everything glows. In the snowy background that is visible through the little window appears a ruddy light.

She is speaking to Fray Diego. . .

You will see, my Father, how it happened. I had desired to see the beauty of a soul that is in the state of grace. While I was longing for this, they commanded me to write a treatise on prayer, though few things that obedience has commanded me have been so difficult as this. The eve of the Most Holy Trinity, while I was praying to the Lord, He spoke through me, He gave me the theme for the book. He showed me a very beautiful globe, formed of a single diamond or of very clear crystal, like a Castle with seven mansions and, in the seventh, which was in the center, was the King of Glory with very great splendor, Who was infusing supernatural light and was making beautiful even those mansions near the inclosure of the Castle. And the light that issued from the palace where the King was, came in greater degree to the mansions that were nearer, but did not pass to the inclosure, and beyond it, all was shadows and darkness, filthiness, great toads and vipers and other noxious creatures.

As I was astonished at the great beauty of the soul that is in the state of grace, and its great capacity, the Lord was pleased that I should see what this Castle is, resplendent and beautiful, this oriental pearl, this tree of life, when it falls into a mortal sin. Therefore the light was suddenly taken away, and although the same sun that used to give it such great splendor and beauty was still in the center of the soul, the crystal underwent a change and was covered with darkness, as though a very black cloth had been placed over it, and it remained ugly, like pitch, and with an insufferable stench; and the noxious things that were outside the inclosure had freedom to enter the Castle.

Believe, my Father, that if we well understood what a soul is like when it sins mortally, it would not be possible to sin. . .

Throughout the account Fray Diego feels that an angel is speaking to him.

And when, presently, having taken leave of the Mother, he found himself alone in his room trying to sleep, the sleep kept fleeing from his eyes.

And he kept thinking:

"If the book of the *Mansions* was born in the Mother thus, well can she say what she declares, that this jewel of the *Interior Castle* has many advantages over the other one of the *Life,* since the silver-worker that made the latter did not know as much then, and that it is gold of finest karat and is fashioned with the most delicate enamellings and designings."

A Page of the "Mansions"

ALREADY the nuns of St. Joseph of Toledo have heard their Mass and during the Mass all received Communion. Now each one in her cell returns thanks to God.

A hot morning of June. In the convent the air is burning. All the cells exhale the heat of love, and the morning light that laughs in the cloister is the joy of the nuns who are rejoicing with the Beloved.

Mother Teresa also is in her cell. She is on her knees beside the stone ledge of the window, but she is not praying. She is writing. She has begun the first line of the book.

María del Nacimiento, who brings a message for the Mother, enters. The Mother takes off her spectacles with both hands and settles herself to hear the message.

María del Nacimiento speaks. . . But what unusual attention on the part of the Mother. She remains with her hands upraised and the spectacles in her hands.

The nun finishes speaking, but the Mother continues listening. What can it be that she is hearing?

María del Nacimiento remains a little apprehensive and looks at the Mother. The Mother is enraptured. . . Her hands upraised and the spectacles in her hands. Before her, the notebook, and in the notebook . . . a miracle!

The nun sees it, but it seems to her that she is dreaming. The sheet of paper that the Mother was beginning is now completely written in her own handwriting. The letters, the words, have appeared of themselves, like flowers of light. . .

It is a page from the *Book of the Mansions*.

VI.

A Woman Restless and Roving

The life of the discalced nuns of St. Joseph seems an anticipated beatitude. The Mother has enjoyed four years of an ineffable and pure happiness. With her poverty, with her daughters, with Christ, she is completely happy.

But not all the souls of Christ are doves of the dovecot of St. Joseph.

There are also doves of Christ out yonder without a dovecot, and sheep of the Good Shepherd without a sheepfold. And the birds of prey fly near and the wolf hovers about.

The soul of Teresa begins to grow restless with an anxiety that impels her, she knows not whither. The heart beats against her breast, seeking outlet for the vehement eagerness of an indefinable solicitude. Fever of love and fever of conquest. Christ . . . the Church . . . souls.

Lord, what do you wish that I do?

THE DUST OF HER SANDALS

Here am I, a poor discalced nun, without aid on any side, except the Lord, charged with commissions and good desires and with no possibility of putting them to work.

But "the love of pleasing God and faith make possible what is not possible according to natural reason."

Again the grating of the cloister is opened and the nun returns to the world.

But this one who returns to the world is Teresa, Foundress and Reformer.

A restless woman! A roving nun!

The Long Road

A ROAD.

An interminable road, in which are joined all the roads of Spain. One day this road is dust that irritates and sun that burns; another day it is a ravine fashioned by a torrent from the clouded sky or mud from the heavy shower or snow from the snowfall.

A road "not easily passable."

Along the road, the cart, and, in the cart, the Mother with four or five nuns.

In front, on mules or on beasts of burden, a clergyman—Julián de Avila—and one or two friars—Gracián, Gregorio Nacianceno, Fray Pedro de la Purificación.

Mule boys on foot or mounted on the beasts that draw the cart.

The cart is a convent.

With the awning and the mantles which hang

behind and in front, it has all the privacy of the monastic cloister.

Within this cloister the traveling Community fulfills its rule. The little nuns spin and sew and pray. An hour-glass which the Mother carries in her knapsack indicates the hours, and a little bottle of holy water banishes the devil.

When the hour-glass marks the hour for prayer, a little bell rings and all keep silence. The clergyman and the friars take the breviaries. The nuns say the hours of their Office. The mule-boys eat and drink in order to swallow better the words that tickle in their throats. The Mother is very careful to see that at these hours they have plenty to eat and drink. In spite of that, this enforced silence is not the least painful part for the boys.

But the little bell rings again and the chatter breaks forth.

The journey is a happy one.

The Mother "talks of God," and even "those

who are accustomed to go swearing and behaving improperly" enjoy hearing her.

Then the journey is pious and lighthearted, like a devout pilgrimage. The music of the little fountain that springs up near the road expresses the joy of the merry company of pilgrims.

But on the bad days, when the sun parches, when the rain drenches, when the snow drifts...

The mother exhorts and encourages, like a valiant captain of soldiers.

"Have much courage, for these days are very rich for winning heaven. . .

And all are encouraged.

But once there was one who answered her: "I was winning it also in my own home. . ."

The Squire of the Lady

Julián de Avila wrote very proudly:

"With these motives and intentions, the Mother left the new monastery of St. Joseph to go to that of the Incarnation, I accompanying her as her squire and as her chaplain. From that day when I offered myself as such, up to the present, I have been her squire and chaplain, and will be so until death."

Proud claim of the fortunate Julián.

It was for some time that this chivalrous and roving Lady had a squire at her service.

"From that day. . ."

The day on which Julián de Avila offered himself to the mother as chaplain and squire was that memorable day of the foundation of St. Joseph. Julián himself calls it the "day of palms". And such it was. A true Palm Sunday. In the morning, the triumph and the

the rejoicing of the new Monastery. In the afternoon, the beginning of a dolorous Holy Week.

That very afternoon, "without further consideration," the Prioress of the Incarnation sent to command the Mother that she should leave immediately the monastery which she had founded, and should return immediately to her own house of the Incarnation. . . Upon hearing the command of the Prioress, the Mother went at once to the Incarnation, leaving alone the four poor maidens just given the habit.

In the passion of the Mother, the road from St. Joseph to the Incarnation was her *via dolorosa*. On this bitter journey Julián de Avila for the first time accompanied the Lady as her faithful and valiant squire.

But another Squire had by that time already taken the lead of Julián de Avila.

* * *

Doña Teresa was still a nun of the Incarnation. One night the nuns sang matins and were leaving the choir for their cells.

Doña Teresa also went out. Together with her comes from the choir her cousin, Doña María de Cepeda. Doña Teresa moves along slowly, slowly. Now she has stopped as though she was conversing. The conversation is not with her cousin.

Doña María also stops, without knowing why. Finally Doña Teresa says:

"Oh, Sister! If you but knew the Squire whom we have, how delighted you would be!"

Doña María answers:

"Let her who knows it tell who the Squire is."

Doña Teresa says:

"Christ with the cross on His shoulders."

Chronicles

ON THE road to Medina del Campo, one morning of the August of 1577, went Teresa de Jesús from Avila. In carts covered with awnings, seven nuns accompanied her. At the side of the carts, some muleboys on foot. A gentleman on a mule, Julián de Avila.

The first adventure of the Foundress. She is fifty-two years old.

The walls of Avila fell behind, and before the eyes of the nun was opened the heroic land of Castile as a country for conquest.

But this field was small for the ardent conqueror. The great love that impels her is not satiated in Castile, nor in the two Castiles, nor in Andalusia. All the roads of Spain will feel the caress of her discalced feet.

* * *

Candid and devoted chroniclers, Julián de

Avila, María de San José, Ana de San Bartolomé,
wrote the story of the Mother's journey. In
their relations, artless and delightful, is clearly
revealed, without artificial adornments, the
heroic achievement of Teresa. The narration is
like a fountain, natural and rustic, from which
flows the clear water. And there is in these relations such sympathy that it is difficult to choose
when one wishes to copy a fragment.

From Julián de Avila, we shall copy the story
of the trip to Salamanca:

> I shall relate here only what we endured
> on the road to Salamanca. As it was warm
> and the sun made our holy Mother ill, we
> left Avila almost at nightfall, and about the
> beginning of the journey, before reaching
> Martín, Fray Antonio, who now was with
> us, had a hard fall from his mount. God
> was pleased that no harm was done in these
> nor in many other falls that He has permit-
> ted on other journeys pertaining to the Or-
> der. The waiting-maid of a lady was with

us. A little farther on, I saw her fall. As it was getting very dark now, because the night was quite advanced, the ass on which was packed the money that was being brought to Salamanca and other securities of the journey, was lost, and did not reappear throughout that entire night, so that, with the falls and the seeking for the ass and with the great darkness, it seemed to me that when we reached the inn, it would be after midnight. Consequently I did not wish to dine, although I'm sure there was need of it, but in order that I might not fail to say Mass in the morning, I had willingly to remain fasting. In the morning a boy went to hunt the lost ass and found him a little apart from the road, for no one had touched him, nor was a thing of what he carried missing. With this, we longed for morning, to go to say Mass at a hermitage that is called Our Lady of the Vineyard. We arived there at a seasonable time, but there was no provision in the hermitage for saying Mass. I had to go to the village, which is at some distance from the hermitage, for the document, and I did not find the priest in the village; there was no one who might give us the document.

Finally, with goings and comings, the whole morning passed, and I, quite against my will, remained without saying Mass and without dining and without lunching, and satiated with traveling. And although the holy Mother remained without receiving Communion, though the journey did not forbid this, I did not feel that so much as I felt what touched myself; because still my work in this matter did not suffice, but they kept laughing at me and with reason.

On another night our loss was greater than that of the ass, although they said he was carrying five hundred ducats. As we were traveling, also by night and in complete darkness, the party was divided into two groups; he who was with the holy Mother, though for the sake of his reputation I do not wish to say who he is, left her and the lady Doña Quiteria, who now is prioress of the Incarnation, in a street of a little village, that they might there await the other group in order that all might be united and might not be separated. Going to seek the others, when they appeared, he that had left them to seek these others returned, and couldn't find the place where he had left them, and, as it was so dark, he became confused in such a way that however many turns he made, he did not find them, and, declaring that they must have gone with those who were farther ahead, we went on for a long time until we were all united. Some of us kept saying to the others:

"Is the Mother coming there?"

They kept saying:

"No!"

"Isn't she coming with you?"

"Why, she was coming with you. What has happened to her?"

In such a way we were completely in darkness, that of the night, which was bad enough, and that of finding ourselves without our Mother, which was much worse. We were uncertain whether to turn back or to go forward. We began to shout, but there was no reply. We had to separate again, some to seek what we had lost, the others to shout to see whether from some distance there might be a reply to us. After a long time of distress for us and of trouble for him who had left them, and of going back over the same road, here was our holy Mother, coming with her companion and a laborer, whom they had brought from his house, and to whom they gave four reals to guide them to the road, and he was the most fortunate because he returned to his house very much satisfied with the money, and we much more so with all our treasure found again, and glad enough to go on, telling our adventures.

* * *

María de San José is that nun whom the Mother herself one day very affectionately called "a lettered woman."

The narrative of the lettered woman is witty and lively.

The nuns listen to it at recreation "in the shade of a beautiful poplar."

The nuns have asked María de San José to tell them about the Mother's trip to Seville, and the lettered nun tells it thus:

> The whole trip was passed laughing and composing poems and couplets about all the events that happened to us, which our Saint enjoyed singularly, and used to thank us a thousand times because with so much pleasure and contentment we endured such great hardships, for there were more than those that I shall relate here; since I do not wish

to be tedious, I shall tell only a few that
gave us most anxiety of mind, such as that
of crossing the Guadalquivir, where we
found ourselves in great difficulty because,
after all the people had passed to the other
side of the river, wishing to take the carts
across, either because it was necessary to
change the course of the boat through consideration for them, or because the boat-
man did not know how to manage, the boat
was carried away with the great force of the
water, and brought a cart or two with it
down the river, so that it seemed that we
were helpless, and already night was almost
upon us and we had enough trouble, for one
reason, because of the shortage of carts,
since without them we were not able to
travel; for another reason, we were a league
and a half from any inhabited place; for
another, it can be imagined how the carters
and boatment would take this event, who
began to discourse according to their cus-

tom, without anyone being able to pacify them. When our Mother saw this, she began to arrange the convent and take possession of it, and it was under a cliff, on the bank of the river. Understanding that we would remain there that night, we began to take out our household furniture and equipment, which consisted of a statue and holy water and books; we sang compline and in this way we spent the time that the poor men were working, fastening the boat with a rope, although our help also was necessary and we began to pull on it, for it almost carried us all away. Finally, as our holy Mother was there, and her prayer was so wonderful, Our Lord was pleased that the boat should stop where it was checked and there was a place to bring it back, and so, well on into the night, we ended by getting out of this difficulty and getting into another, which was to lose the road and not to know what direction to take. A gentleman who, from a distance had seen our troubles of that afternoon, sent us a man, who assisted us greatly, although at first he kept saying a thousand abominable things about friars and nuns, without being moved to set to the work for which he had been sent. I do not know whether it was on seeing us pray that he was moved in such a way that he aided us with much charity, and even as he was leaving, when we had again lost the road, he showed it to us, going thus half a league with us, and asking our pardon for what he had done.

Another day we passed through Cordoba, awaiting permission to bring the carts across by the bridge, which was given with a thousand difficulties, and so were there many other occurrences of troubles and obstacles which our Mother considers as insignificant. We reached Ecija the third day of the Feast of the Holy Ghost; we took the road to a hermitage of the glorious St. Anna, which was outside the town, where we heard Mass, went to confession, and received Communion, and because there was a kindly feeling there, in order to be retired, our Mother wished to remain and to have the door of the hermitage closed upon us; she commanded that the people should go to the inn and that something should be sought that we might eat; we stayed thus until two o'clock without anybody returning, and when they came at this hour, they brought us from the town lettuce, radishes, and bread, which we ate very contentedly. Our Mother declared that on no journey or foundation had there happened to her that which happened on this one, spending so many days without finding anything with which to provide for her nuns; I do not know whether it was because of the slight skill of those that had to provide it, or whether the Lord wished that the hardships which had to be endured in this foundation should be begun.

This day, with the pretext that she was ill, our Mother did not wish us to keep her company, as on other days, but she was alone all day, without consenting that we speak to her, enclosed in a little sacristy that was there, where she employed herself well seeking new services to perform for the Holy Ghost, on Whose feasts the ardent love that she had for this Divine Spirit showed plainly, as is clearly seen by a paper that I have, written in her handwriting, where also is expressed that friendship and union which the Lord made between her and our Father Gracián, and that vision which she said she had had in Veas. Because I have written both the one and the other else-where, I do not speak of it now; but of the fact that in this hermitage, where we were this day, she made a vow of obeying every day of her life the said Father Gracián, in all that which should not be contrary to the obedience due her superiors. . .

The journey to Burgos was similar in unforeseen disasters and misfortunes, to the trip to Seville.

The traveler is now old and stooped. Sixty-seven years old. But the same flame of fire, which in her youthful years inflamed her with eagerness to conquer, still burns and transfigures the wrinkled flesh of her old age.

The chronicler of this last heroic deed is that fortunate lay-Sister who, by a miracle of the Mother, learned to write in Salamanca.

María de San Jerónimo has preserved the story of Ana de San Bartolomé:

> Traveling along the bank of a river, we found the mud so deep that it was necessary to alight, because the carts were sticking in the mud. Then climbing a hill, having left this danger, we saw before our eyes another much greater, and it was that the holy Mother saw the cart in which her nuns were riding overturned in such a way that they were on the point of falling into the river,

and the hill on which we were was so rough that there was not room for many people to gather in order to free them or check the cart so that it would not fall. At this point I saw a youth among those we brought with us, who seized the wheel and held the cart so that it would not fall, but he seemed the Guardian Angel rather than a man, because it was not possible for him to hold it alone, if God did not free them.

It gave our holy Mother enough anguish to see this, because it seemed to her that her nuns were going to be drowned, and from the time that she saw this, she wished to go ahead, so that she might be the first in the other dangers that might present themselves. And for rest from this trouble that had passed, we came that night to an inn where it was not possible to make a bed for our holy Mother, and despite this scant shelter, still it seemed that it would be well for us to stay here some days because of the information they gave us about the condition of the road, for the rivers were so swollen that the water was more than half a yard over the bridges. The innkeeper was such a good man and had so much pity for us that he offered to go ahead in order to guide us through the water, because, as it was so turbulent and the bridges were covered, the road along which we had to go could not be seen. These wooden bridges were so nar- ow that the wheels barely fitted on them, so that we were in danger of falling into the river if they should deviate even a very little. Before entering upon the danger we went to confession and asked our holy Mother to give us her blessing, like people that were on the point of death! And also we said the Creed. The holy Mother, when she saw us so disheartened, agreed upon some things with us, and as she had more faith that Our Lord had to withdraw us successfully from this danger, she kept saying to us with much joy: "Come, my daughters! What more do you wish than to be martyrs here for the love of Our Lord?" And she said, furthermore, that she would pass first, and that she would request us not to go further, if she should drown, but to return to the inn. At last, God was pleased that we should come out safely from this danger.

With these troubles our holy Mother was so ill and her tongue was so thickened with paralysis that it was a pity to see her. We came to a village before noon and then she managed that the Father Povincial should go to say Mass; she communicated at it and then her tongue was loosened and remained better. From here we went to Burgos that night and we met with such high water that the streets were like rivers. The lady who was awaiting us, hoping to lodge us in her house, is a person of such great charity that she had a very good fire for us, and lodged us very well.

As our Mother was so drenched, she stayed longer at the fire than she was accustomed; it made her so ill that that very night it gave her a dizziness and such severe nausea that, as she had an inflamed throat, it caused a sore wound so that she spat up blood, and on the following day she could not get up to conduct business, but was placed on a cot, which they put at a window on the corridor where were those who talked to her."

Let us, for the present, cut short here the chronicle of the lay-Sister. Later we shall again apply to her, that she may tell us the true conclusion of this story, the divine nuptial song of Alba de Tormes.

Inns and Taverns

IN THE journeyings of the Foundress, the inns and taverns have a pleasant and real similarity.

The Inn of the Hunger, the Inn of the Bishop, the Tavern of the Star, the Lodging of the Carnation and of the Blood. . . Inns and taverns of the two Castiles, of La Mancha and of Andalusia.

Still a halo, venerable and half sacred, envelops them. Perhaps one day at the hour of scorching heat, the nomadic cart of the roving nun stopped at their door. Or one night at an untimely hour, Julián de Avila made their large knocker resound. And still there has not died away in their pebbled entrances the sound of the sandal of the nun who crossed over them.

* * *

The fact is that on these journeys the taverns and inns were the torture of the Mother. Julián de Avila says:

"As for what there was good in these inns, we couldn't wait to see ourselves out of them."

And María de San José adds:

"The most usual thing was to remain in the fields, surrounded by the people who accompanied us, in order to escape the confusion of the inns and taverns. And so we left the carts as seldom as possible."

But the Mother was not always able to shun the martyrdom of the inns. In them, amidst the rough voices of the muleteers and the coarse conversation of soldiers and students, she more than once prayed the psalms of her breviary in the light of the kitchen lamps.

The figure of the Mother in the inns is attractive. And the life that she led in them is interesting. She tried, naturally, to follow as closely as possible the orderly and austere life of her beloved convent. And sometimes she achieved it. Fray Diego de Yepes relates an encounter he had with the Mother in an inn of Arevalo, which for her really was peaceful and monastic:

[161]

"While I was traveling the road from Medina del Campo to Zamora, she happened unexpectedly to go from Medina to Avila with three nuns, and God was pleased that she should come to lodge at the same inn where I was. I gave her my room, which was the best that there was in the inn, and I served as their porter in order that they might be at more liberty in their recollection, and after they had had their hours of prayer, we spent a very great part of the night in conversation about heaven. It was agreed that in the morning I should say Mass for them and give them Communion in the Church of St. Francis, but the day dawned with so much snow that neither we nor they were able to leave Arevalo. They heard Mass and received Communion, as was agreed, and, returning to the inn, they spent all that day in the recollection usual in their monasteries. . ."

Further on we shall hear some "excellent things" which the Mother let fall from her lips in the conventual peace of this inn.

But more frequently the inns were for the Mother a real purgatory. In them she used to suffer with her daughters the most unusual hardships. Of this kind were the inns on the road to Seville, which María de San José describes.

". . . Coming to an inn outside Cordoba," writes the nun, "the first day of the Feast of the Holy Ghost, so terrible a fever afflicted our Mother that she began to rave, and the only coolness and protection that we had for so terrible a fever and so severe a sun, which was increasing it, was a little room in which, I believe, there had been pigs, with a roof so low that we were hardly able to stand erect, and so wretched that the sun entered through a thousand holes, and we had to set this room apart with our mantles and veils; the bed was such as our Mother indicates in the book of the Foundations, and she remarks only on this and not on the multitude of cobwebs and insects that were there. All that was in our power to remedy it was done. But it was what happened during the time that we were there, with the cries and oaths of the people that were in the inn and the torture of the dances and tambourines, without any pleas nor gifts being sufficient to make them leave from over the head of our Mother, who, with the fury of the fever, was, as I have said, almost unconscious; finally we decided it was advisable to take her out of there and to leave, even though it was the hottest part of the day. . ."

* * *

In another inn, still more infernal, the Saint stopped on this same journey. The same María de San José paints its scenes:

Having left Ecija, we continued our journey until we arrived at Seville, with no less trouble than had happened to us in the past. And I shall finish with the last day, when we arrived at an inn at noon, Wednesday of the four ember days of the Most Holy Trinity, where we found for food only very salty sardines, with no water to

drink. So great was the difficulty in which
we found ourselves from the thirst which
the sardines caused that, seeing this difficulty and that there was no water, we
stopped eating. The heat was excessive and
our Mother was in the cart, which was near
a rubbish heap, where the sun was so strong
that it seemed to burn us; we who were
coming with her and those who were in another cart asked permission to get out and
to be together near the door of her cart,
thinking we would feel the heat less;
finally, we made some protection against the
sun with some mantles of coarse frieze, and
hoped to be more secluded from an endless
number of odious people who were in that
inn and near it, who gave us much more
trouble than all those whom I have mentioned, for unless you should see it, you
could not believe that there were such de-
testable people among Christians. Our ears
could not listen to the oaths and the curses

and the abominable things that those disso-
lute people were saying, who, having finished eating, became violent; nor do I know
whether the lack of water caused it. Finally they drew their swords and began such
a conflict that everything seemed to over-
whelm us, and we looked into the Mother's
cart to seek shelter with her, but although
at first, when they were gambling and
blaspheming, she had been much disturbed,
she was now laughing, with which we consoled ourselves, for now it seemed to us our
end had arived. She understood that the
tumult was caused by the demons in order
to disturb us, and it stopped immediately
without any one having been wounded, and
there were more than forty swords, and we
had also heard harquebuses discharged, and
all this in the hands of a crowd furious and
without judgment, moved with infernal
fury. Oh, what great rage the demon used
to show against the holy and valiant woman.

This was the life of the Foundress in inns and taverns. It is not strange that, on speaking of the sufferings of mortal life, she should compare it to a night in a bad inn. Well she knew what bad inns were.

Dawn

THE Mother has left Malagón on the journey to Villanueva de la Jara. This entire journey is a triumphal march. The towns of Mancha take a holiday at the passing of the Mother. The little bells of the mules that draw her cart sing out, and it is as though the bells of the towers are set flying in a peal of glory on the feast of the Resurrection. Or as if there were heard the clinking of the silver awning the day of Corpus Christi.

The crowd, exhilarated, kneels when the Mother passes, that she may bless it. It seems that it is Christ who passes.

When she enters the house in which, among a hundred, she chose to rest, the multitude knocks at the door and invades the room through the windows. There is a tumult and some end in the prison.

A rich farmer has gathered together his children and his flocks in order that the benediction of the Mother may fall upon all of them.

Through the flat prairie that has been converted into a waste land advances a procession of discalced friars, who come to receive her. The friars humbly kneel and ask her blessing.

Another procession more gleeful and clamorous. Children. . . When they reach the Mother's cart they kneel with their hoods off. The Mother blesses them. Arranged in two rows, they bring the Mother to the church. They sing and shout.

On this triumphal journey, the Mother one night agreed with her followers to leave very early on the following morning, to escape the tumult of the people. Three hours before dawn the mules were already yoked. The carts squeaked through the narrow streets but the town did not awake.

"Praised be God," said Fray Antonio de Jesús, "that now we travel in peace."

"This morning," added Fray Gabriel de la

Asunción, "there will not be a reveille of horn-pipes and flageolets, like that of yesterday."

And it is true, this morning there is no reveille of hornpipes and flageolets. But there is another reveille. In the sky, white with moonlight, quiver the stars, rejoicing. From up yonder descends a most exquisite music, that pierces the Mother's soul. It seems as though the stars were singing. As though the whole heaven were a luminous foliage, and the stars were nightingales that warbled in their nest of light.

The music is a hymn of thanksgiving—thanks to the Mother for the hardship of this journey of twenty-eight leagues.

Ana de San Bartolomé also hears the music.

And hearing it, she thinks:

"What a saint, God help me, what a saint! When they fail to praise her on earth, the heavens extol her and sing to her."

The Frying-Pan

ONE Catalina de Tolosa, a great friend of the Saint, has presented to the Mother much household furniture, consisting of beds and many other things, in order to establish and prepare the foundation at Burgos.

The same good friend has bequeathed to the convent an income for the maintenance of the foundation. But a scruple has come to the Mother in regard to this income, and she has renounced it before a notary public.

As a result the monastery is now so poor that the nuns have nothing to eat.

And the worst of it is that in the city the fact of the income from Doña Catalina is known, but the fact of the renunciation is not known. And since everybody thinks that the monastery is well provided, no one will take care of sending alms to the nuns.

But the Lord will take care of them.

Already He is beginning to take care of them.

A lady calls at the turn and gives to the Mother an alms of one hundred *reals*.

A hubbub of rejoicing in the convent. An alms of one hundred *reals* is certainly enough to excite the nuns. At the hour of recreation, a chapter to determine the first thing that must be bought. In this chapter all have a vote, Tomasina Bautista, Inés de la Cruz, Catalina de Jesús, Catalina de la Asunción, and even the little Sister with the white veil, María Bautista.

Sister portress says first there must be bought a curtain and gratings for the turn, for all this is needed.

Sister sacristan asks for wine cruets and some altar cloths and candles, and I don't know what more for the church.

Sister wardrobe-keeper wishes serge for habits and coarse linen for the straw beds.

Sister cook has no pepper, no caraway seed, no salt, no cumin seed.

Sister María Bautista says they are greatly in need of brooms in order to sweep, for the ones that Doña Catalina gave are now quite worn out.

Finally all the nuns have given their opinions. Now, the requisite vote of the Mother. The Mother looks at all of them and smiles to herself.

"The first thing, my daughters, is a frying-pan for the kitchen."

Astonishment among the nuns. As the chapter is held in jest, a protest is begun.

Sister cook declares:

"As for the frying-pan, my Mother, a good old woman who is our neighbor lends one to us every day."

But the Mother is not convinced:

"Remember, my daughters, that at profession we offered to the Lord the condition of being poor, but not the annoying of our neighbors. . . The frying-pan, the frying-pan."

The Last Journey

ALONG an interminable road across the desolate, bleak plateau of the Moraña of Avila the Mother goes journeying. Long leagues that never end.

She left Burgos courageously and arrived at Medina with the longing to go to leave her bones in the little dovecot of Avila. But in Medina obedience changed her route, obedience so rigorous that the Mother never felt so much "anything that the prelates might command her." But she obeyed and took the road to Alba de Tormes.

Cruel journey. Old and bent, her staff no longer sustains her, and in a corner of the long, narrow cart she huddles under the awning of canvas, tanned by dust and sun. It is the last journey. But it seems that in it have been gathered all the fatigues and all the sufferings in order to make this final journey the most dolorous for the Mother.

When it seemed finally that the labors of Burgos had been ended, the Mother asked the Lord: "Lord, are You now content?" And the Lord answered her: "Go, for another greater work now remains for you to endure." The Mother did not then understand what work the Lord was announcing, but she knew it well when those miserable little villages, neighbors of Peñaranda, did not have an egg to give her to eat.

Let us give what Ana de San Bartolomé tells us:

> We went from here, from Medina, in a large coach that took the road with such great difficulty that when we came to a little village near Peñaranda, the holy Mother was enduring such pains and weakness that a fainting fit caused her, that it made us all pity her to see her, and we didn't have a thing we could give her for this, except some figs, and with that she remained

that night, because not even an egg could be found in the whole place. Now, I being afflicted to see her in such great need and not having anything with which to help her, she kept consoling me, saying that I should not mind, because those figs were more than good enough, and that many poor people did not have so much luxury. She said this to console me, but as I now knew the great patience and suffering that she had, and the joy that it was to her to suffer, I believed her suffering to be greater than she made known, and in order to remedy this necessity we went another day to another village, and all that we found to eat was some cabbage boiled with plenty of onions, of which she ate, although it was very bad for her illness.

It is the exile that, at the end, is made most painful and cruel.

But the Fatherland is near.

They are distant five leagues from Alba de Tormes.

VII.

"Now This Little Butterfly Is Dead"

The white butterfly flies, flies over the last sandy waste of the desert.

It seems that the little star of that light, which she alone sees, calls her and attracts her.

It is the red gleam of the Heart of Christ.

Christ has opened His breast and, through the aperture, begins to appear the crest of flames of his Heart. This is the light. This is the rosebush.

The butterfly flies toward the glowing fissure. She rests her wings upon the breast of Christ.

Now indeed we can say that this butterfly died finally with the intense joy of having found repose, and that Christ lives in her.

The Spouse Comes

ON THIS autumnal morning the bells of the convent of Alba are quivering in their small belfries, with a pealing of glory.

From the bed of the river comes the harmonious sound of the water which, this morning, on running over the dike of the mill, sounds with the mighty music of a triumphal march.

The trees of the poplar grove also join their boughs and weave under the illuminated vault of the heavens triumphal arches.

The Carmelite monastery is wholly enveloped in a golden cloud of Ascension Day.

And, in the borders of the garden, the little autumn flowers tremble rejoicing, like little Sisters, who wish to join hands in order to dance with joy.

The Spouse comes.

Mother Teresa awaits Him in her cell.

Mother Teresa is dying.

"NOW THIS LITTLE BUTTERFLY IS DEAD"

The little dove, white and stainless,
    Wings her way, returning now,
To the ark of safety, bearing
    In her mouth the olive bough.
Now her melancholy cooings
    Will the turtle dove abate,
On the verdant banks rejoicing
    In the presence of her mate.

At seven of the morning she turned herself on one side with her face toward her daughters, who were kneeling about the bed.

She fixed her eyes on the crucifix that she held in her hands, and remained in prayer.

She is wounded.

This is the "restless woman," nightmare of Nuncios.

This is the ecstatic and visionary nun, torment of the easily frightened theologians.

This is the reformer of iron, the hammer of all relaxation.

This is the writer.

This is the pilgrim.

[181]

And this is also the "little white dove" that flew so much.

No longer does she fly.

Love has singed her wings, and, burned in His immortal fire, she has fallen on this "green bank" of the Tormes.

And Love is finishing consuming her above His fire.

*   *   *

And Love transfigures her.

Her face is very beautiful and inflamed with so great a beauty that greater has not been seen in her life; it is not known where the wrinkles have hidden, for she had many because of her age and of her infirm health. . . She seems illuminate. . . Her face, like a glowing sun.

Come, O Spouse, come.

The Spouse does not hold the lighted lamp in her hand.

All of her is a nuptial lamp of fire and wholly an oil which, burning in the lamp, is consumed.

"NOW THIS LITTLE BUTTERFLY IS DEAD"

At nine o'clock at night, Ana de San Bartolomé, who was at the head of the Mother's bed, saw a luminous cloud that filled the cell. The splendor enveloped the body of the Mother.

And, in the cloud, as on a throne, was seated the Most Holy Trinity.

The Mother inclined her head, moved her lips, and gave a sigh.

> I stayed and I forgot myself,
> I reclined my head upon the Beloved,
> Lost to all things and to myself,
> Leaving my cares
> Forgotten among the lilies.
>
> O night that has shown the way,
> O night, lovelier than the dawn,
> O night, that united
> The Lover with the Beloved,
> The Beloved transformed into the Lover.

* * *

At this point a simple man came in, a servant of the house, and after having kissed her feet, before all, he raised his voice, and striking his hands together, declared:

"God help me, ladies, how the feet of this saint have the fragrance of citrons, lemons, oranges, and jasmines. . ."

Panegyric

BLESSED is this little butterfly that has died at last. Now she is the Mother in heaven. She was yet living on earth and her life and her deeds were the theme of public sermons. Sometimes the preachers rebuked her and condemned her as a public sinner. Other times they praised her as a canonized saint. Persons of such rank as the Papal Nuncio said of her most abominable things, "terrible accusations of things so grave and evil that even hearing them could not be endured." And serious and learned men published very great encomiums of her.

The opprobriums were for her the "cause of much interior joy," and the eulogies humiliated and mortified her.

But now, since she is in heaven, no longer is she able to feel concern over the praises. We

can, then, make her panegyric without danger
that it might wound her humility.

The best panegyric of the Mother is the testimonies of those who best knew her.

Let us commence with the testimony of María
de San Jerónimo.

She was a cousin of the Mother, but the love
of a relative does not blind her, because she is a
discreet and serious nun. A good proof of her
discretion is her having been Prioress in Avila
and in Madrid, and foundress in Ocaña. On
speaking of her cousin, she knows well what she
says, because she herself has seen it in her inter-
course with the Mother, and, besides, she has
many times heard her great friend, Ana de San
Bartolomé, speak of it.

Of her many commendations, let us choose
those which refer to the virtue of penitence, so
beloved by the Mother.

"She used to have," says the nun, "great longings for penitence, and with this she was always
seeking inventions to do more, but with having

great infirmities, there was no progress being made and so one day she agreed with the Sisters that all of us should dress in coarse frieze, and that we should wear it in place of the serge that we now wear next to the body, and that the sheets and the pillow cases should be of this material, and with this she said that she was to be the first who would put it on and so she did, because she said that if it did harm, that she wished to try it first before the Sister should put it on, and she wore it, and all of us did likewise until the superiors commanded that it be taken off, because they said it was very bad for the health. In using disciplines and haircloth, she exceeded to such a degree that she inflicted wounds on herself."

The greatest eulogies that have been published of the Saint are, perhaps, those that Fray Pedro Ibáñez wrote about her.

The holy Mother one day affectionately called this Father "this Dominican Father of mine." He, in turn, called himself the "son" of the

Mother. And it is true that when he speaks, his voice seems tender and sweet as that of a son and serious and authoritative as that of a father.

Then with this love of a father and of a son, Fray Pedro weaves a long series of eulogies. Let us now see a few:

> She has great purity of soul, great chastity, fervent desires of pleasing God, and, in exchange for this, of trampling under foot all that there is on the earth.

> No one deals with her who, unless he has a depraved disposition, is not moved to devotion by her, although she does not speak of these things.

> She has so firm an intention of not offending the Lord, that she has made a vow of omitting nothing that is more perfect unless he who judges it should say to her that she should not do it, and, although considering as saints those of the Company, and it seeming to her that by their means Our Lord has given her so many graces, she has

told me that if she did not know that it was greater perfection to deal with them, that never would she ever speak to them nor see them, although they are the ones who have calmed her and directed her in these things.

God has given her a soul that is so strong and valiant that it is astonishing. She used to be timorous, now she tramples under foot the demons. She is very far from the fastidiousnesses and childishness of women; very much without scruples, she is very direct.

All her conversations, her letters, her actions, are full of humility, desiring greatly that all the world should see her past faults and miseries and should speak of them, being also very much disturbed that they should consider her good. And at the beginning, when the gifts of God began to increase in her, she was dying for fear lest anyone should comprehend anything about them, in order that they might not suspect that she was good. Never has she had self-confidence, despite her having very good understanding; she has always wished to be governed by the opinion of another.

The purity of conscionce of this Religious is so great that it astonishes those of us who have heard her confession and given her Communion, and her companions, because it can be said that all she thinks of and treats of is God. Everything is directed to the honor of God and to spiritual progress; and there can under no consideration be any venial sin, however small it may be, if she understands it to be evil.

More restrained but perhaps of greater authority is the other Dominican, Fray Domingo Báñez, in the eulogies of the Mother. His praise, judicious and measured, has all the prestige of the Master of Prime of Salamanca.

When he speaks, the timid theologians who condemned her are silent.

Fray Domingo, then, says:

I have always proceeded with caution in the examination of this relation and of the prayer and of the life of this Religious, and no one has been more incredulous than I in what pertains to her visions and revelations, although not in what pertains to her virtue and good desires; because of this I have great experience of her truthfulness, of her obedience, penitence, patience, and charity toward those who persecute her, and of other virtues, which anyone who wishes to deal with her will see in her; and this it is which can be esteemed as a more certain sign of the true love of God than the visions and revelations. And I do not underrate her revelations and visions and ecstatic raptures, rather I suspect they could be from God, as they were in other saints, but in this case it is always safer to be fearful and cautious, because in feeling security, the devil has a place to deal his blows, and that which before was, perhaps, from God, will be changed and will be from the devil.

The end of this *panegyric* we have reserved for a witness of rank. It is that Fray Diego de Yepes, who was the first brother Prior and then Bishop of Tarazona. He had such great knowledge of everything pertaining to the Mother that he wrote her biography. He himself says:

"I knew her for many years, she wrote me many letters of great edification, she told me purposely some graces that God gave her because she thought to help me in this, and I carefully gathered other things that fell from her hands carelessly."

Let us hear one of these things that fell from the Mother's hands while she was speaking with Fray Diego:

A year before she died, when I was questioning her with the freedom that I, as a son, had, she told me that she was engaged in perpetual prayer and never was withdrawn from the presence of His Majesty, nor wished for more than the fulfillment of His divine will. I, as an unpolished fellow and one without experience or feeling of those graces, said to her: "That condition has to change." She answered me that it would not change and that it had been fourteen years since the Lord had put her in that state and that it was for the same length of time that she had not been having ecstacies because, if they had lasted, her life would already have ended; but that He communicated the same delights to her without ecstasies, that she used to experience in them. She had them to a very great extent in the beginning; it used to happen to her, only upon hearing the name of God, to remain for long periods enraptured; and, reading at night the lessons of the matins, with this name alone to remain standing so with the light in her hand, until God should let her return to her senses. . .

We shall not prolong this panegyric further. Let us trust that it may have been agreeable to the holy Mother, since these preachers who have praised her were all such good friends of hers.

She will not dare to censure these as she censured those that did not please her because they had "much brains" or because they did not preach purely for the sake of God and of souls, but with a consideration of human purposes, because they were, for example, "opposed to some house of canons."

Portraits

IF YOU wish to know—who can help but wish it?—what the face of the Saint was like, look at these portraits of her that remain to us.

Fray Luis de León was consoled with seeing and knowing the Mother "in two living images that she left us of herself, which are her daughters and her books."

Certainly these portraits are valuable for revealing imprinted in them the spirit of the Foundress and of the Writer; but we wish also her corporal image.

A worthy lay-Brother, Fray Juan de la Miseria, "great servant of God and very simple in the things of the world," was once painting in Seville.

He finished painting a door and set himself to portray the Mother Teresa.

It is no slight martyrdom for her to let herself be painted. She would prefer that after her death there should remain of her in the world neither name nor face nor memory.

But within a few days the Mother has to return to Castile and these daughters, who remain in Seville, will no longer have other comfort except this portrait which Fray Juan is going to paint.

Furthermore, Father Gracián has commanded the lay brother to paint her, and the Mother to let herself be painted.

And the Mother obeys.

The nuns, crowded under an arch of the cloister, look at her, amazed. María de San José, Prioress, ventures to say:

"Look at her, daughters, see how beautiful she is."

She is seventy-one years old. But her body, mortified by sickness and by penance, maltreated by the sun, by the cold northerly wind, by the dust of the roads, still shines with an unfading beauty. The interior light of the ecstasies blooms in her eyes and in her face, and all the flesh of her body reflects as a divine lamp of crystal, always enkindled in order to go forth, at any hour, to the meeting with the Spouse. And the sun, this Andalusian sun, that, on the road, used to fall on her as a fire, envelops her now in a halo of light and of gold.

But this Fray Juan de la Miseria is not very excellent, nor is he a very considerate painter. He was once painting an Ecce Homo. For lack of other model, he put a nun before him. But the nun was pale and the painter needed a model stained with blood. Fray Juan seized the hands of the nun, knotted them firmly, and watched how the blood burst forth vividly.

Nor is he very courteous with the Mother now. He fulfills his office without niceties nor courtesies. He takes her face with his large, ugly hands of a lay-Brother and twists it from one side to the other until he finds the inspiring light that his brush seeks. The Mother laughs sometimes, but Fray Juan rebukes her, and she, obedient and submissive, regains the gravity of features that the artist requires for the painting.

Finally, the Mother laughs freely. And, laughing, she says to Fray Juan:

"God forgive you, Fray Juan, for now that you have painted me, you have painted me ugly and blear-eyed."

*   *   *

The work of Fray Juan de la Miseria did not wholly satisfy Gracián.   He would wish that the picture of the Mother had been more lifelike, because she "had a very expressive countenance which used to move to devotion."

Catalina de Cristo, also, says that the picture which Fray Juan has painted "somewhat resembles" the Mother, but that she has " a more beautiful face with very benevolent eyes and very fair."

Father Ribera says of her eyes that they were "a little swollen and lively and expressive, and that when she laughed, her whole face laughed and showed joy."

[198]

The brushes of the "little friar" have not had the delicacy necessary to paint those eyes and that face and those hands. The nuns complain of poor Fray Juan de la Miseria. And María de San José never wearies of looking at the Mother with fixed and long glances, with much love.

The Mother finally left Seville. She struggled, suffered, traveled, and died in Alba de Tormes. The Carmelites weep without consolation. María de San José wishes to console her daughters in Seville and for this purpose is going to show them a portrait of the Mother. Not the one by Fray Juan de la Miseria, but another more like her, which she herself will paint. To paint it, she has, instead of a pencil, her "lettered" pen. Here is the portrait of the Mother that María de San José painted:

This Saint was of medium stature, rather large than small; she had in her youth the reputation of being very beautiful, and even her old age showed it; her face was not at all usual, but extraordinary and of such a kind that it could not be described as round nor aquiline; it was perfectly proportioned, the forehead wide and smooth and very beautiful; the eyebrows of dark red color, with a slight appearance of black; wide and somewhat arched; the eyes, black, bright and round, not very large, but very well placed; the nose rounded and on a line with the lachrymal caruncles above, diminishing until it became even with the eyebrows, forming a pleasing space between the eyebrows, the tip rounded, and a little inclined upward, the nostrils slightly arched and small and not very much raised from the face. The perfection which she possessed in every feature can be but poorly described with a pen. The mouth of very small size. The upper lip thin and straight, the lower lip full and a little drooped, of very pretty grace and color, and as she had color in her face, although she was now old and had many sicknesses, looking at her and listening to her gave much pleasure, because she was very courteous and gracious in all her words and actions; she was plump rather than thin, quite well-proportioned. She had very pretty hands, although they were small; on her face, at the left side, three raised moles, like little warts, in a straight line one from the others, beginning below the mouth, the one that was largest, and another between the mouth and the nose, and the last on the nose more nearly under than above. She was perfect in everyway, as is seen by a portrait that Fray Juan de la Miseria produced, without art.

*　　*　　*

These are the portraits of the Mother that her two children painted. The two painted her as beautiful. But neither the brush of the lay-Brother nor the pen of the nun was able to reveal a divine beauty that the Mother concealed under her pure flesh, behind her forehead, deeper than the abyss of her eyes. . .

[201]

. . . That secret beauty, which the eyes of the Lover saw in her:

THE LOVER: Thou hast wounded My heart, My sister, My spouse, thou hast wounded My heart with one of thy eyes, and with one hair of thy neck.

THE SPOUSE: "By that single hair that fluttered
    On my neck and seen by Thee—
Thou did'st look again upon it
    And wert by it drawn to me.
Thou wert made a willing captive,
    Weak and slender though it be,
And I dared to look upon Thee,
    And in looking wounded Thee."

THE LOVER: Behold thou art fair, O My love, behold thou art fair, thy eyes are as those of doves.

THE SPOUSE: "While on me Thine eyes were resting,
    Full of sweet and gracious love,
They impressed on me their beauty;
    Heavenly beauty from above.
Then Thy love flowed in upon me

"NOW THIS LITTLE BUTTERFLY IS DEAD"

And mine eyes obtained the
grace
What they saw in Thee to wor-
ship,
O the beauty of Thy face.

I was once unclean and swarthy,
In a miserable plight;
Yet I pray Thee not to spurn me,
Or to cast me from Thy sight.
Of my former degradation,
There remaineth not a trace,
For Thine eyes have rested on me,
Shedding comeliness and grace."

PRINTED BY BENZIGER BROTHERS, NEW YORK